ADHD

WHAT EVERYONE NEEDS TO KNOW®

ADHD

WHAT EVERYONE NEEDS TO KNOW®

STEPHEN P. HINSHAW
AND
KATHERINE ELLISON

OXFORD
UNIVERSITY PRESS

OXFORD
UNIVERSITY PRESS

Oxford University Press is a department of the University of
Oxford. It furthers the University's objective of excellence in research,
scholarship, and education by publishing worldwide.

Oxford   New York
Auckland   Cape Town   Dar es Salaam   Hong Kong   Karachi
Kuala Lumpur   Madrid   Melbourne   Mexico City   Nairobi
New Delhi   Shanghai   Taipei   Toronto

With offices in
Argentina   Austria   Brazil   Chile   Czech Republic   France   Greece
Guatemala   Hungary   Italy   Japan   Poland   Portugal   Singapore
South Korea   Switzerland   Thailand   Turkey   Ukraine   Vietnam

Oxford is a registered trademark of Oxford University Press
in the UK and certain other countries.

"What Everyone Needs to Know" is a registered trademark of
Oxford University Press.

Published in the United States of America by
Oxford University Press
198 Madison Avenue, New York, NY 10016

Library of Congress Cataloging-in-Publication Data
Hinshaw, Stephen P.
ADHD : what everyone needs to know / Stephen P. Hinshaw and
Katherine Ellison.
pages cm
Includes bibliographical references and index.
ISBN 978-0-19-022379-3 (pb : alk. paper)—ISBN 978-0-19-022380-9
(hb : alk. paper)   1. Attention-deficit hyperactivity disorder.   I. Ellison,
Katherine, 1957-   II. Title.
RJ506.H9H58 2015
618.92'8589—dc23
2015014400

1 3 5 7 9 8 6 4 2
Printed in the United States of America
on acid-free paper

We dedicate ADHD: What Everyone Needs to Know® *to anyone who has ever wondered whether the occasional joys of spontaneity are worth the annual costs of replacing lost sunglasses, keys, and cellphones, and to everyone willing to make the effort to understand, appreciate, and occasionally forgive the blessings and challenges of neurodiversity.*

CONTENTS

ACKNOWLEDGMENTS   xiii
INTRODUCTION   xv

PART I: FACING THE FACTS

1   What Is ADHD? And Why Should We Care?   **3**

In a Nutshell, What is ADHD?   *3*

What are the Core Symptoms?   *4*

Is ADHD Best Considered a Deficit of Attention? Or is the More Basic Problem a Lack of Self-Control?   *8*

Aren't the Symptoms So Often Attributed to ADHD Simply Typical Characteristics of Being a Young Child (Especially a Boy)?   *10*

What's the Difference Between ADHD and ADD?   *11*

What are Some Good Reasons to Take ADHD Seriously?   *12*

Focusing On: The Nature of ADHD   *13*

2   How Widespread Is It?   **15**

How Prevalent is ADHD in the United States Today, for Both Children and Adults?   *15*

How Fast Have US Rates of ADHD Been Increasing, and Why?   *16*

Do the Rising Rates of ADHD have Anything in Common with the
Similarly Rising Rates of Autism?   19

Is this Disorder Something New or Has it Always Been Around in
Some Form?   20

Focusing On: Prevalence   24

3. What Causes It?   **25**

What is the Most Common Cause of ADHD? (Spoiler Alert: It Runs in
Families)   25

What Other Factors Might Cause ADHD?   27

What's Going on inside the Brains of People with ADHD that
Causes the Symptoms?   30

How Much Influence Do Parents Have, if Any—And in What Ways?   33

What Role Do Schools and Academic Pressures Play in Today's
High Rates of ADHD?   37

What Do People with ADHD Need to Know about Video Games, Social
Media, and Other Forms of Screen Entertainment?   38

Focusing On: Causes   41

4 How Do You Know If You Have It?   **43**

Under What Circumstances Should Your Child, Your Partner—Or You
Yourself—Be Evaluated for ADHD?   43

Who is Most Likely to Diagnose ADHD?   44

How Should ADHD be Diagnosed?   45

Why Do the Symptoms Show Up More Often in School and on the
Job than at Other Times?   48

Is There Any Objective Assessment for ADHD, Such as a Blood
Test or Brain Scan?   49

What Do You Need to Know about the Diagnostic and Statistical
Manual (DSM)?   50

What is Neuropsychological Testing, and is it Ever a Good Idea?   52

What Kinds of Professional Guidelines Exist for the Diagnosis of ADHD?   53

What Kinds of Problems or Conditions Produce Symptoms Similar to ADHD, and How Can Clinicians Distinguish Which Issue or Issues to Treat First?   54

What Additional Disorders or Life Problems Commonly Coexist with ADHD?   58

Are there Special Considerations for Diagnosing the Inattentive Form of ADHD?   61

What Can You Do to Make Sure You Get the Best Possible Assessment?   62

Focusing On: Diagnosis   63

5. How Does ADHD Change Over the Lifespan?   **65**

What Does ADHD Look Like in the Earliest Years of Life?   65

What are the Typical Consequences of ADHD in Grade School?   66

How does ADHD Reveal Itself During Adolescence?   69

To what Extent Does ADHD Persist into Adulthood?   71

How does ADHD Influence People's Self-Esteem?   72

But Wait! Isn't ADHD Really a Gift?   73

What Contexts Best Suit People with ADHD?   75

What is the Evidence for Resilience in People with ADHD—that is, the Chance for Positive Outcomes Despite the Symptoms?   76

Focusing On: ADHD Over the Lifespan   76

6. How Much Does It Matter Who You Are and Where You Live?   **79**

How Do ADHD Rates Vary Between Males and Females?   79

How Do the Symptoms Vary Between the Two Genders?   80

What are the Long-Term Consequences of ADHD for Females, Especially When the Disorder isn't Addressed in Childhood?   81

What are the Differences in Diagnoses Among Racial and Economic Groups?   84

What Accounts for the Increased Diagnoses Among Racial Minorities and Low-Income Groups in Recent Years? 84

How Much Do Rates of Diagnoses Differ Among US States, and Why? 86

How Much Do Rates of ADHD Vary Among Nations Outside the United States? 88

What are the Implications as ADHD Diagnosis and Medications Become International Phenomena at Increasing Rates? 89

Focusing On: Differences Among Groups 90

PART II: TAKING ACTION

7 How Helpful—or Harmful—Is Medication? 95

How Many US Children and Adults are Taking Medication for ADHD? 95

What are the Most Common Stimulant Medications in Use? 96

When and How Did Doctors First Begin to Treat ADHD with Medication? 97

How Do Stimulant Medicines Work to Help People with ADHD? 98

What are the Chief Pharmaceutical Alternatives to Stimulant Medications? 101

What are the Side Effects of ADHD Medications? 102

Can Taking Powerful Stimulant Medications at a Young Age Harm a Developing Brain? 103

What are the "Ritalin Wars"? 104

How Long Do Medication Benefits Last? 106

Why Do So Many Teens with ADHD Stop Taking their Medicine? 107

How Should Doctors Monitor Treatment with Medications? 108

How Can Patients Improve their Chances of Effective Medication Treatment? 110

How Might Taking ADHD Medication Influence Later Risk for Substance Abuse? 111

How Likely is it that People Who Take ADHD Medications Will Become Dependent on Them or Abuse Them? 112

How Much of a Problem is Abuse of ADHD Medications Among People Who Don't Have the Disorder? 113

How Do Other Countries Compare with the United States in Medication Prescriptions for ADHD? 116

Focusing On: Medication 117

8 How Helpful Is Behavior Therapy, and What Kinds of Behavior Therapies Help the Most? 119

What is Behavior Therapy? 119

What is Direct Contingency Management? 120

What Can You Expect from Parent-Training Programs? 121

How is Behavior Therapy Used at School? 125

How Effective are Social Skills Groups for Children and Adolescents with ADHD? 127

What Kinds of Programs Can Help Kids with ADHD Get More Organized? 128

What is Cognitive-Behavior Therapy, and can it be Effective for ADHD? 129

Which is Best, After All: Medication or Behavior Therapy? 130

Focusing On: Behavior Therapy 131

9 What Other Strategies May Be Helpful in Treating ADHD? 133

What Do We Know About the Value of Daily Exercise? 133

How Does Diet Affect ADHD? 135

Which Supplements, if Any, Are Worth a Try? 137

What is Neurofeedback, and How Helpful is it for People with ADHD? 140

Beyond Parent Management Therapy, What Other Help is Available for Families Coping with ADHD? 143

What Kind of Academic Support is Available from Schools? 145

Focusing On: Additional Treatment Strategies 148

10 What Do You Need to Know About the "ADHD Industrial Complex"? 149

What Do We Mean by the "ADHD Industrial Complex"? 149

What are Some Particularly Egregious Examples of Schemes to Avoid? 150

Can Marijuana Cure Distraction? And—Are We Pulling Your Leg by Even Asking? 153

How Helpful are Computer Training Programs? 154

What is Coaching, and How Much Can it Help People with ADHD? 156

How Useful are Other Alternative Treatments for ADHD? 157

What, if Any, Evidence Supports Mindfulness Meditation for ADHD? 158

When Might it Make Sense to Enlist an Occupational Therapist? 159

How Can You Be a Smart Consumer? 159

Focusing On: The ADHD Industrial Complex 161

11 Conclusions and Recommendations 163

Can America's Rate of ADHD Diagnoses Continue to Grow? 163

How are Big Pharmaceutical Firms Influencing the Surge in ADHD Diagnoses? 166

What Impact, if Any, Have State Policies Had in the Rise in Diagnoses? 168

What Needs to Be Done to Foster Greater Understanding of the Reality of ADHD in Girls and Women? 170

What Do Today's High Rates of ADHD Say about Our Culture? Is this a Warning Sign We Need to Address? 171

What Would Some Sensible, Evidence-Based Policies Look Like to Prevent Overdiagnosis and Underdiagnosis and Most Effectively Cope with ADHD? 173

Focusing On: The Future 175

RESOURCES 177

INDEX 181

ACKNOWLEDGMENTS

We are grateful to Oxford University Press for recognizing that ADHD merits a place in the *What Everyone Needs to Know*® lexicon. In particular, we deeply appreciate the support and guidance of our editor, Sarah Harrington, and the enthusiastic efforts of Andrea Zekus regarding all aspects of publishing this book. Katherine Belendiuk and Elizabeth Owens gave us excellent suggestions from their careful reading of the text.

Steve gives perennial thanks to Kelly Campbell and sons Jeff Hinshaw, John Neukomm, and Evan Hinshaw for their support and love.

Katherine thanks Jack Epstein, as always, and sons Joey and Josh Epstein.

INTRODUCTION

Attention deficit hyperactivity disorder (ADHD) seems to be everywhere these days. In recent years, the number of diagnoses has skyrocketed. More than 6.4 million US youth—amounting to one in nine children between the ages of 4 and 17—have now at some point in their lives received a diagnosis of ADHD, according to a major national survey of parents. That's a *41 percent increase* in the numbers of such diagnoses in less than a decade. The disorder has recently become the second most frequent diagnosis of a chronic condition for children, after asthma.

Newspapers, TV, and blogs provide constant coverage of the apparent epidemic. Few classrooms lack one, two, or more diagnosed students. Nor is ADHD merely for kids: Adults with the disorder are now showing up at medical clinics in record numbers.

ADHD provokes fierce controversies—as much as if not more than any other mental condition. Critics go so far as to deny it exists, disparaging it as an excuse for anything from bad parenting, lazy kids, and stifling schools to a society intolerant of individual differences. People are fiercely divided over the practice of treating its symptoms with powerful stimulant medications. Some skeptics even portray ADHD as a lucrative conspiracy between psychiatrists and pharmaceutical companies. Defenders counter by pointing to the disorder's well-established biological roots and to prodigious research clearly revealing that untreated ADHD often devastates lives.

Ambiguity adds to the general confusion. Although ADHD is most often a serious impairment, in some cases it may be a source of strength. As is the case with other forms of mental disorder, from depression to schizophrenia and from anxiety disorders to autism, scientists today know a great deal about the causes, mechanisms, and potential treatments for ADHD, but to date have no objective way to diagnose it.

In the meantime, ADHD has become a hallmark of our data-swamped and increasingly competitive era. Since the dawn of the Information Age, children and adults alike have been struggling to navigate a rising deluge of information and choices that challenge our slow-evolving brains. Students are being educated in classrooms that on average are growing more crowded, more diverse, and more pressured to achieve, ever earlier and ever faster. All of these relentless changes in our society and economy have made distraction, forgetfulness, and impulsivity—all classic symptoms of ADHD—common complaints.

There's widespread concern, particularly among parents, about whether ADHD unfairly stigmatizes boys. Although boys and girls alike may be impaired by the disorder, boys are much more likely to be diagnosed at an early age, as their symptoms are often more disruptive at home and in the classroom. At this writing, *one in five* American boys has received the diagnosis by the time they surpass elementary school. And even as this alarming statistic suggests that some clinicians may be too quick to diagnose boys, many girls who need treatment are slipping under the radar—as are boys who are more distracted than hyperactive—risking serious long-term harm to both their mental and physical health.

By far, however, the keenest controversies concerning ADHD have to do with the common practice of treating the condition with powerful pharmaceutical stimulants. Nearly 4 million US children—roughly 70 percent of those currently diagnosed—now receive such medication. Despite government approval and doctors' assurances that the drugs are safe and effective in curbing serious distraction and impulse-control problems, many people worry about the efficacy of such treatment and whether the medications might be harming young minds. More broadly, many fear that as a culture, we're grasping for quick fixes to address vexingly complex social problems.

As we've only fairly recently come to understand, adults as well as children are grappling with the consequences of ADHD. Just a few decades ago, scientists presumed that ADHD symptoms ceased at puberty. Yet researchers and clinicians have since documented that even though much of the fidgeting and hyperactivity diminishes by the teen years, other ADHD symptoms (particularly inattention and poor organization) persist into adulthood in half or more of all childhood cases. Today, scientists estimate that nearly 10 million adults meet the criteria for the disorder, with rates of adult diagnosis rapidly increasing. As increasing numbers of adults find their way into treatment, they've become a large new market for medication. Young and middle-aged women have become the fastest-growing market for such prescriptions.

We predict that, for the next few years, the numbers of both young and adult Americans diagnosed with ADHD will keep rising. The reasons for this trend are varied, but one of the most important factors is the continuing increase in both awareness and acceptance of the disorder. Moreover, for the last quarter-century, an ADHD diagnosis has provided a ticket for accommodations and special services in school. It can also garner payments from Medicaid and other health insurance programs. As a general rule, when conditions are explicitly linked to services and funding, their rates of diagnosis will often rise beyond their actual prevalence.

Another major reason for the climb in ADHD rates lies in the increased pressures throughout our society for ever greater performance in classrooms, offices, and factories—and such pressures certainly aren't going away anytime soon. More fuel for the rise in rates comes from doctors who are diagnosing ever-younger children. Key professional groups, such as the American Academy of Pediatrics, now urge that diagnosis and treatment begin as early as age 4, in order to head off the risk of years of failure. Meanwhile, early childhood education is gaining in both popularity and public funding throughout the United States, leading to increased demands on many more youngsters to control their behavior in school settings.

On the other hand, the current rates of increase can't continue indefinitely. We foresee that rising concern about overdiagnosis and abuse of ADHD medications will eventually lead to more rigorous diagnostic procedures and an eventual downturn in the rates. It's just not likely to occur anytime soon.

Whereas once ADHD was considered a mostly American phenomenon, awareness, diagnosis, and treatment have been growing in other nations. Increasingly, children are being diagnosed in every nation with compulsory schooling, at rates that are surprisingly similar throughout the world. International rates of medication for ADHD are also starting to approach those in our country, causing similar controversies, although America remains the clear leader of this trend.

While critics raise alarms about the risks of medication, we're learning more and more about the enormous costs to taxpayers of untreated ADHD. Beyond the direct costs of treatment and of special education programs in school, Americans end up paying hundreds of billions of dollars every year in indirect expenses for juvenile justice programs, substance-abuse management, expenses connected to accidents, and the huge toll of low work productivity for adults. Added to this financial burden is the more intimate pain involved in personal and family hardships, including the high rates of academic failure, rejection by peers, joblessness, unfulfilled lives, and divorce that have been linked to ADHD.

Both the biological roots and often devastating impacts of ADHD have been established throughout decades of research and supported with tens of thousands of peer-reviewed, published studies. Some of America's leading scientific researchers have dedicated their careers to investigating the basic brain mechanisms governing attention, self-control, and organizational ability, as well as optimal treatment strategies and the mechanisms that underlie their success. Even so, American opinion remains sharply divided—and, all too often, misinformed and confused—over the nature of ADHD and the reasons for this seeming epidemic.

Several valid questions have emerged that demand thoughtful answers. Do the escalating numbers of children diagnosed with attention problems point to broader problems with an educational system that demands that children sit still for hour after hour as they cram for standardized tests? Has the label at least in some cases become a ruse by which parents (or college students, or employees) can game the system for accommodations? Are all these new prescriptions encouraging drug abuse, including the use of ADHD medications as study aids by college and even high school students who don't have the disorder but who are desperate for any kind of edge?

These justified concerns, together with the ignorance and skepticism, add to the burden of stigma shouldered by people who have the disorder. All mental disorders incur shame and discrimination, but the questions over the authenticity of ADHD too often lead to blaming those who pursue help. Medication is often viewed as a crutch, a chemical band-aid attempting to cover family conflict, poor school performance, or more general social problems. The result is that many individuals and families who genuinely need help have not pursued it.

In other words, in many cases ADHD is being *underdiagnosed* and *undertreated,* as people are persuaded by critics or scared off by the controversies. Some avoid getting a diagnosis altogether, while others turn instead to what we call the "ADHD industrial complex," a maze of aggressively touted but unregulated supplements, special schools, and counseling, where it's easy to waste money and precious time.

Simultaneously, ADHD is surely being *overdiagnosed* in a growing number of cases, in part due to the increasing availability of government benefits. These changes have resulted in greater numbers of poor children than ever before being diagnosed with this disorder—helpfully for some but not so helpfully for others. Moreover, as life in the new millennium becomes ever more competitive, many Americans, including people in the workforce and many students, are seeking to gain advantage in pills that promise greater focus and less need for sleep. Many, including worried parents and unscrupulous adults, are willing to fudge symptoms in order to obtain a diagnosis; even more are able to buy the pills illegally.

Fueling the overdiagnoses are the quick-and-dirty ADHD assessments all too often made by nonspecialists, in office visits lasting fewer than 15 minutes. Even the most respectable professionals, who are trained to provide accurate diagnostic workups, may find themselves rushing through the process due to a lack of adequate reimbursement. To the extent that the medical establishment and our society in general fail to take ADHD evaluation more seriously, we'll all be paying the price.

All this explains why, in the following pages, we aim to transcend the polarization surrounding too many discussions of ADHD and provide straight talk and sound guidelines for educators, policymakers, health professionals, parents, and the general public. This book will include an explanation of the core symptoms of ADHD, its biological origins and dynamics, and its varying rates among males and females, various ethnic groups, and between US states and internationally. We'll detail some of the most exciting recent scientific breakthroughs about the nature of ADHD, explaining how both children and adults are affected by the disorder and how the nature of ADHD changes as people's brains develop. You'll learn how school policies and other pressures for performance are fueling today's fast-rising rates of diagnoses. We'll also provide a guide to intervention strategies, including medications and psychosocial therapies as well as practical information about how parents and teachers can help children struggling with the disorder. We'll tell you how to choose a professional who can advise you on a sound plan for assessment and treatment. At the same time, we'll emphasize throughout these pages that any consideration of ADHD must take into account both underlying biology and sociocultural forces. Rather than *either-or*, the issues are *both-and*.

ADHD: What Everyone Needs to Know is the product of a collaboration between University of California psychology professor Stephen Hinshaw, an international expert on ADHD and mental health in general, and Katherine Ellison, a Pulitzer Prize–winning journalist and author who in recent years has focused on writing and speaking publicly about ADHD. Both of us bring powerful personal as well as professional experience to this task. Hinshaw, who grew up with a brilliant father who suffered severe but misdiagnosed mental illness, has dedicated his career to understanding the combination of biological, family-related, and school-linked factors related to childhood mental health and its treatment and has published extensively in this field. His most recent book, coauthored with his colleague Richard Scheffler, is *The ADHD Explosion: Myths, Medication, Money, and Today's Push for Performance.* Ellison, who was herself diagnosed with ADHD as an adult and has a son with the disorder, has devoted the past decade to investigating and writing about ADHD, other learning disorders, neuroscience advances, and education policy. She is the author, among other works, of *Buzz: A Year of Paying Attention.*

To help with your own focus as you read along, we summarize each chapter at its conclusion, in sections titled "Focusing

On. . . ." We also ask you to keep in mind these general, key points:

- *A diagnosis of ADHD marks the starting point for an educational journey—some might call it a forced march—that above all requires an open mind.* Despite all that scientists now understand about the genetic and biological origins of mental disorders, these ailments emerge in the context of early life experiences and remain much more difficult to define and cure than organ failures, injuries, and infectious diseases. Separating fact from fiction about ADHD is no easy task, given the unusual controversies and misinformation surrounding the disorder.
- *Mental disorders rarely occur in isolation—rather, they are typically accompanied by comorbidities, a fancy name for related maladies.* Serious comorbid conditions that can result from or coexist with ADHD include anxiety, depression, and oppositional behavior, as well as learning disorders and Tourette syndrome. As children grow older, other problems may also emerge and coexist with ADHD, most commonly substance abuse, eating disorders, and self-injurious behavior. These add-on problems may eventually overshadow the core problem of ADHD, requiring considerable attention and additional treatments.
- *In the world of ADHD, biology meets context head-on.* Although there's no doubt about the biological origins of ADHD, the nature and severity of the symptoms unfold in interactions within families, classrooms, and peer groups. Certain symptoms may yield considerable impairment in certain families, schools, and jobs, but not so much in others. Thus, we must always take into account not just the individual's underlying biochemistry but also his or her upbringing, social relationships, occupation, and the level of support received in school or on the job.

- *No discussion of ADHD can ignore the role of school policies and pressures.* This is especially true given that ADHD symptoms typically become problematic during the first years of schooling, when demands for attention, self-control, and academic performance multiply.
- *Finally, saying that someone "is ADHD" rather than "has been diagnosed with ADHD" is a grossly misleading, meat-cleaver way of reducing a person to a highly variable facet of his or her personality.* In other words, go ahead and label the condition, but don't label the person. We don't call individuals "autistics" or "schizophrenics" or "manic depressives" any longer, for good reason: In order to genuinely empathize with people who deal with the consequences of mental disorders, we need to separate the person from the condition. One of our greatest hopes for this book and for both of our related professional endeavors is to reveal the many ways our society stigmatizes mental illness, including subtle jokes, lowered expectations, discriminatory policies and—often most harmfully—the tendency for people who are labeled as mentally ill to believe in these stereotypes, despair, and stop trying. Having ADHD is hard enough; going without support can make it impossible to bear.

Together with the other titles in the *What Everyone Needs to Know®* series, this book is intended to be a concise guide rather than an encyclopedia. More exhaustive coverage of many specific aspects of ADHD appears in some of the resources listed at the end of the volume. Our aim is to provide you with an overview of the most authoritative and up-to-date scientific knowledge available, with reminders of the potential for human suffering or hope involved at each step of the way.

PART I
FACING THE FACTS

1

WHAT IS ADHD? AND WHY SHOULD WE CARE?

In a Nutshell, What is ADHD?

ADHD, the acronym for attention deficit hyperactivity disorder, is a neurodevelopmental problem that can result in distraction, forgetfulness, impulsivity, and in some cases excessive, restless physical movement, from fidgeting to pacing.

That said, ADHD doesn't comfortably fit in a nutshell. It is a complicated condition of variable origins and dynamics that can show up in markedly different ways from person to person and throughout a person's lifetime. One basic rule, however, is that ADHD typically emerges in childhood, although in some people—many of them girls—it may escape recognition and diagnosis until their teens or even adulthood.

ADHD is not so much a problem of uniformly poor attention or fidgetiness as it is of *poorly regulated* attention and action. The behavior of people with ADHD varies, sometimes dramatically, over the course of an hour, a day, and a school year (or work year). Indeed, many individuals with ADHD can focus extremely intensely—even obsessively (a phenomenon known as "hyperfocus")—when they're intrinsically interested in what they're doing.

Like depression, anxiety, other mental illnesses, and even high blood pressure, ADHD is a spectrum disorder. You can have some of the symptoms at low or moderate degrees of severity and not qualify for a diagnosis. Most if not all of us are at least occasionally prone to being distracted, restless, and impulsive, particularly if we're tired or overly stressed. It's only when the symptoms reach a critical mass, producing impairment in more than one context—for example, both at home and at school—that a diagnosis is warranted. In a world of ramped-up pressures within classrooms and offices, where consistency of self-control is at a premium, this disorder can become a major handicap.

What are the Core Symptoms?

The most common and problematic symptoms of ADHD are forgetfulness, distractibility, lack of focus, restlessness, and impulsivity. More than other people, children and adults with ADHD often have trouble keeping track of directions and conversations. They procrastinate instead of finishing work that doesn't interest them and often end up with rushed, messy final products that don't reflect their creators' skills and talents. They forget where they put their homework, sunglasses, and keys. (At the end of each school year, parents of students with the disorder often discover overdue homework, buried in backpacks, from months before.) They may often feel impatient and be easily bored, and can seem careless, and unintentionally (usually) rude. People with ADHD often ignore risks that are obvious to others and wittingly or unwittingly defy social norms. They may interrupt someone who's talking, impulsively pick the first response on a multiple-choice test, and blow out the candles at other children's birthday parties.

The problems characteristic of ADHD fall into two groups, the first being symptoms of inattention and disorganization and the second involving hyperactivity and impulsivity. The former group of symptoms can make it seem that individuals with ADHD don't really care what others are saying or doing, yet the problem is more likely that they're failing to follow the thread of the conversation—a particularly serious issue when it comes to directions given by teachers or bosses.

The latter group of behaviors can make people with ADHD seem self-centered, reckless, and frenetic. But as we highlight in later chapters, these behaviors related to distraction, sensation-seeking, and excessive movement may actually reflect various means of staving off boredom and compensating for a brain that values immediate gratification rather than a more judicious focus on long-term benefits.

Clinicians refer to three types—or "presentations"—of ADHD: the *inattentive* form, which makes it hard for people to sustain focus and ignore distractions; the *hyperactive/impulsive* variant, in which people experience chronic restlessness and problems in inhibiting impulses; and the *combined* type, in which, just as it sounds, there's a combination of both kinds of symptoms. Scientists studying ADHD believe that a majority of people who have the disorder have the inattentive form. Most who get diagnosed, however, have the combined form. That's because visibly hyperactive children and adults stand out more and are often more annoying than spacey daydreamers. It's much more likely in their cases that a teacher, parent, spouse, or boss will notice the problem and encourage the person to get help. (Typically, only very young children, mostly preschoolers, are diagnosed with the purely hyperactive-impulsive variety. As they grow up and are obliged to pay closer attention to tasks in school, they normally end up diagnosed with a combination of inattention and impulsivity.)

The *Diagnostic and Statistical Manual,* or DSM, the American mental health profession's official guidebook (see more about the DSM in Chapter 4), lists typical symptoms of the inattentive variety of ADHD as distractibility and forgetfulness, making careless mistakes, and having trouble sustaining focus, including when trying to listen to instructions, finish tasks, and organize materials. People with this subset of symptoms also tend to avoid tasks that take a lot of work and to forget where they put things. The hyperactive/impulsive subset includes such symptoms as excessive fidgeting and tapping, trouble staying seated, running around (or, for adults, having a restless mind), talking excessively, blurting out answers, and having difficulty waiting one's turn.

For young children (preschoolers up through the early elementary grades), the core problems are typically related to overactivity and defiance toward parents and teachers, compared with other children their age. By the middle of grade school, children with the disorder often have difficulty listening to teachers and following their increasingly complex directions. It's at this age, additionally, that conflicts with peers multiply. In secondary school, when students are first obliged to switch between classes and teachers during the day, children with ADHD may be handicapped by their disorganization. For those individuals with ADHD who make it to college, the intense academic demands can be overwhelming. By adulthood, difficulties in managing requirements on the job and close relationships often come to the fore.

Scientists have found that people with ADHD struggle in particular with two essential types of cognitive skills: *working memory* and other *executive functions*. Working memory is a vitally important skill that we use all the time. It involves holding two or more things in your mind at once—things as basic as where you're going and how to get there. Poor working memory is why many children with ADHD can't seem to follow multistep directions, such as a teacher's instruction to "Open your history books, turn to page 38, and read the first three paragraphs." A working memory deficit can flummox you during the simplest tasks of daily life, such as trying to figure out why you opened the refrigerator door or keeping track of a conversation. Poor working memory is a strong predictor of academic failure and a major threat to self-esteem.

Executive functions refer to a broader and more sophisticated set of skills, no less crucial to getting along in the world, including the ability to think ahead, plan, organize, strategize, correct errors, and recognize and act on the feelings of others. Deficits in executive functions help explain why children and adults alike who are diagnosed with ADHD have so many social problems and troubles managing their lives. They may forget to show up at appointments or arrive late, fail to keep track of birthdays or other important events in the lives of their closest friends and relations, surrender to their strong temptation to receive immediate rewards, and struggle to pay their bills on time and finish projects. Life without hardy executive functions can be chaotic.

Intriguingly, some people who qualify for a diagnosis of ADHD do not experience significant problems in either working memory or other executive functions. Their inattentive and impulsive behaviors appear to have a different set of brain-based underpinnings, which may have to do more with motivational deficits or early brain disruption due to prenatal complications. They are impatient and impulsive but not because of fundamental problems related to executive functioning. The lesson here is that ADHD is not a single entity: There are several pathways, beginning before birth and early in life and involving different brain regions, that can lead to similar groups of core symptoms and their impairments. (In Chapter 3 we more specifically discuss the causes and dynamics of this complex condition.)

In short, ADHD is defined by patterns of behavior that are far beyond the norm for individuals of a given age range, patterns that betray a forgetful, sometimes reckless, apparently thoughtless, and most often disorganized and erratic style. These behavior patterns are not universally counterproductive; as we'll later explain, a subset of people who meet criteria for ADHD are unusually innovative and creative. Unfortunately, however, it's more common that people with severe ADHD symptoms have serious difficulty adjusting to the demands of daily life, ending up with a track record marked by repeated failures, seriously challenged relationships, and battered self-image.

Is ADHD Best Considered a Deficit of Attention? Or is the More Basic Problem a Lack of Self-Control?

Ever since 1980, the name for this complex syndrome has included the phrase "attention deficit," yet that phrase only begins to describe the problems that can be involved. For one thing, there are different forms of attention, including *sustained attention* over long time periods and *selective attention*, involving where we choose to focus our mind's spotlight. People with ADHD may vary in which kinds of attention deficits affect them the most.

What's more, some experts contend that by focusing our attention on attention, we might be overlooking the potentially more serious handicap of lack of self-control, otherwise known as willpower, self-discipline, or the ability to delay gratification. Abundant research over the past several decades has confirmed the importance of this basic skill not only in avoiding life-long disappointments but also in achieving success.

The pivotal study along these lines was the famous "marshmallow test," designed in the early 1960s by Walter Mischel, a psychologist now at Columbia University. Mischel and his colleagues gave a group of preschoolers an option: They could enjoy one marshmallow (or other favorite treat) right away, but if they managed to wait for 15 minutes, while a researcher left the room, they could have two. In follow-up studies, the researchers found that children who were able to defer gratification and wait for the double reward had better life outcomes well into adulthood, including higher SAT scores, greater academic achievement, and, not surprisingly, lower rates of obesity.

Mischel and his colleagues proposed that for every child or adult attempting to delay instant gratification (with anything from a marshmallow, a cigarette, or a shopping spree), a conflict exists between the brain's opposing tendencies toward impulsivity and restraint. As we pursue long-term goals, we all must find a way to let our cooler heads prevail, suppressing our most impulsive instincts in favor of good judgment. People who manage to do this consistently tend to lead safer, happier, healthier, and more successful lives.

It's clear that many people with ADHD have a harder time than others controlling their impulses, which gets them into well-documented trouble including but not limited to problems with friendships, traffic accidents, drug abuse, gambling, and marital conflict. That's why some experts, chief among them the psychologist Russell Barkley, a major ADHD investigator and theorist, contend that the core problem with the disorder is less one of attention than of successful control of impulses. As he explains, when people lack the ability to control or inhibit their responses, they never even get a chance to deploy essential executive functions, such as working memory and long-term planning. Instead, they're at the mercy of whatever responses were previously rewarded. Thus, in his view, people with primary problems of attention and focus (i.e., those with the inattentive form of ADHD) have a fundamentally different condition than do those whose most serious problem is impulsivity.

Yet another perspective on the core problem with ADHD comes from the pioneering work of psychiatrist Nora Volkow, director of the National Institute on Drug Abuse. Volkow contends that ADHD boils down to a deficit of motivation, or as she calls it, an "interest disorder." She bases this on brain-scan findings (which we detail in Chapter 3) revealing that at least some people with ADHD may be underaroused physiologically, which helps explain why they are chronically drawn to the neural boost of an immediate reward and less willing to do the long-term work necessary to develop important skills. The paradigm of a sleepy ADHD brain also sheds light on why so many people with the disorder are restless and fidgety, as the constant activity may be part of a struggle to stay alert. Some experts use this model to explain why many people with ADHD can be so annoying: They may be teasing, provoking, and demanding, specifically to get a rise out of others, as conflicts can be energizing.

Another deficit area pertains to the tendency for people with ADHD to have problems with time management and organizational skills. They may grossly underestimate the time needed to complete a task, leaving their final performance far short of their intentions and talents. They may also show up late to many meetings, appointments, and even their own children's performances, contributing to perceptions that they're unreliable, insensitive, and uncaring. They may complete their work but lose it or forget to turn it in, making them seem irresponsible, when they're actually trying their best.

See what we mean when we call ADHD complicated? You can *try* to define it in a nutshell, but it takes time to understand the nature of the underlying problems linked to ADHD, which not only vary dramatically between people diagnosed with it but also affect those people differently in different environments and over the course of a single day or year.

Aren't the Symptoms So Often Attributed to ADHD Simply Typical Characteristics of Being a Young Child (Especially a Boy)?

This can be a vexing question. Certainly, hyperactive and impulsive behaviors are legion in toddlers and preschoolers. It takes many years for young humans to obtain a modicum of self-control, as they become socialized and as their brains mature. Scientists have only fairly recently learned that the brain's frontal regions, crucial for self-regulation and executive functions, do not reach full maturity until about age 25. This raises a reasonable concern over whether we're pathologizing childhood itself, and especially boyhood, as boys' brains are generally slower to develop than those of girls.

In this way, ADHD presents quite a different case than autism. The symptoms characteristic of that disorder, including an infant's resistance to being held or establishing eye contact, a toddler's slowness to pick up language, and a slightly older youth's obsessive focus on quirky interests, tend to stand out as developmentally abnormal. The sheer ordinariness of ADHD-related behavior patterns makes diagnosing ADHD trickier but no less essential. As we describe in Chapter 4, a qualified psychologist or psychiatrist or well-trained pediatrician should be able to tell the difference between the typical characteristics of childhood and the extreme and potentially impairing symptoms of ADHD—but only if he or she follows evidence-based guidelines for thorough evaluations.

What's the Difference Between ADHD and ADD?

The short answer is: none. ADHD, or attention deficit hyperactivity disorder, is a relatively new name (as of 1987) for what used to be called ADD, attention deficit disorder.

Now for a bit of background. Many people are confused over this issue, and for good reason. ADHD has had more than half a dozen names in the century over which clinicians have been diagnosing it, a history we'll detail below. It wasn't until a paradigm shift in 1980 that clinicians began to focus on focus (or more specifically, on problems with focus). At that time, the disorder was renamed attention deficit disorder (ADD).

This new name reflected a more compassionate view of the interior lives of the children who were affected, a perspective originally proposed by the Canadian psychologist Virginia Douglas. In the early 1960s, Douglas began working with seriously distracted children at an outpatient clinic at the Montreal Children's Hospital. She was drawn in particular to the boys who couldn't seem to control their impulses, rushing through their schoolwork, making careless mistakes, cursing, fighting, and running through the halls. Douglas gradually developed a theory that the impulsive behavior was rooted in a problem in sustaining attention—a view that would ultimately contribute to the major expansion of the number of children eligible for diagnosis and treatment through the 1980s. At that time, ADD became a blanket term that incorporated both the inattentive and hyperactive-impulsive forms of the disorder.

But in 1987, the revised edition of the official handbook of mental health, the DSM, changed the name once again, to ADHD, encompassing hyperactivity. Although this remains the preferred official name, many authors, speakers, and clinicians still use "ADD" to describe the disorder, while others use "ADD" to refer specifically to the inattentive form of ADHD.

We'll be using ADHD, and recommend that you do, too, to be precise and correct—but we can't guarantee that the name won't be changed again. Some scientists, in fact, wonder whether the condition shouldn't be called an inhibitory deficit disorder or some other term that might more precisely define the underlying problem. For now, remember that ADHD refers to a wide range of underlying deficits and impairments and not simply distractibility.

What are Some Good Reasons to Take ADHD Seriously?

Longitudinal research, in which children with ADHD are monitored over many years, provides crucial answers to this question. The news, after 15, 20, and even 30 years of follow-up, is not uplifting. People with ADHD, a number of investigative teams have found, show significantly more struggles with drugs and alcohol and many more teen pregnancies, car wrecks, suicide attempts, sexual diseases, and encounters with police (and even shorter lifespans) than comparable individuals without ADHD. On average, they also have fewer close friends, less satisfactory marriages, and more frequent vague medical complaints. Hinshaw's team, in particular, has documented striking impairments specific to girls and young women with ADHD, which we will discuss later in this book.

Focusing On: The Nature of ADHD

ADHD is a surprisingly common behavioral disorder, with core symptoms involving distraction, difficulty in sustaining focus, impulsivity, and in some cases restlessness and hyperactivity. Whereas it ranges in severity depending on the individual, the time of day, and the demands involved, it can become a serious disability in many situations, especially including traditional school environments or jobs that prioritize the capacity to sit still for long periods of time and to juggle tasks. ADHD is not a new condition: Serious distraction and poor self-control have existed throughout human history. Yet US rates of the disorder have skyrocketed in recent years, at least in part because of our continuing push for academic and job performance.

2

HOW WIDESPREAD IS IT?

How Prevalent is ADHD in the United States Today, for Both Children and Adults?

Before we answer this question, let's be clear about the difference between a condition's actual prevalence and its diagnosed prevalence. *Prevalence* of ADHD is just what it sounds like: the proportion of people who truly have the disorder, relative to the total population. *Diagnosed prevalence*, in contrast, refers to the percentage receiving a diagnosis from a clinician, whether or not that diagnosis is entirely accurate.

True prevalence is relatively easy to ascertain for medical illnesses that can be detected through specific biological tests, such as HIV—as long as the researchers sample the general population and not just people arriving at clinics. Yet with mental disorders, estimating both the prevalence and diagnosed prevalence is a tricky task, given the lack of objective markers and consequent risks of both underreporting and overreporting. Underreporting may be due, for instance, to fear of stigma by a potential patient (or his or her family) and to a lack of qualified medical professionals to diagnose the condition. Overreporting, in contrast, may occur due to cursory diagnoses, rising pressures for achievement, and the chance that people are seeking to gain an advantage from prescribed medications.

As we explain at length in this book, many factors influence who gets diagnosed and who doesn't, meaning that diagnosed prevalence may be an imperfect barometer of true prevalence for ADHD. Increases in rates of diagnosis may instead reflect medical or societal changes—from increasing awareness about the disorder to government policies that encourage people to seek valuable accommodations. We hope you'll keep these issues in mind as you consider the following statistics.

As we mentioned in the Introduction, approximately 11 percent of all US children aged 4–17 have at some point received an ADHD diagnosis, according to the most recent available survey by the US Centers for Disease Control and Prevention (CDC), covering 2011–2012. This figure translates to approximately 6.4 million US children and adolescents. As for adults, no comparable formal estimates are available, in part due to the historic consensus that ADHD was mostly a childhood disorder. Yet today, clinicians and privately commissioned surveys report that adults are the quickest-growing segment of the population receiving diagnoses and being prescribed medication, with the number of adult women surging especially fast. Researchers estimate that half or more of children diagnosed with ADHD will continue to have significant and impairing symptoms as adults, from which we can deduce that just more than 5 percent of adults are affected. This works out to be approximately 10 million US adults.

How Fast Have US Rates of ADHD Been Increasing, and Why?

The quick answer is *really fast*. We mentioned in the Introduction that the rate of ADHD diagnoses has risen by more than 41 percent over the past decade. A bit of recent history will help place this surprising news in context.

The rate of diagnoses of the disorder now known as ADHD picked up in earnest during the 1960s. A landmark of that era was that the psychostimulant methylphenidate, marketed under brand names including Ritalin (and, since 2000,

Concerta), was first approved in 1961 for children suffering from the disorder now known as ADHD. The demand for diagnoses increased appreciably once parents realized there was a seemingly simple treatment that could help their restless children focus in school.

At that time, scientists estimated that about 1 percent of children had been diagnosed with ADHD, even though there were no reliable national surveys to check the accuracy of that claim. More certain are the increases in the rate of diagnosis over the next couple of decades. The reasons were varied, including the introduction of new diagnostic terms—first ADD in 1980 and then ADHD in 1987—that carried with them new and more expansive criteria. Another boost in the rate of diagnosis came with the emergence of the first community support groups, including what later became Children and Adults with Attention Deficit Disorder (CHADD), a vigorous national lobbyist. We'll tell you more about CHADD and similar groups in Chapter 6, but the upshot is that they not only effectively helped spread awareness about ADHD but also catalyzed some major policy changes in the early 1990s.

One such innovation was the 1991 reauthorization of the Individuals with Disabilities Education Act (IDEA), the federal government's special education law, initially passed in 1975. After its reauthorization, IDEA included ADHD as a specific diagnosis that could qualify a child for special services and accommodations. At roughly the same time, Medicaid coverage was expanded to include a greater number of childhood conditions, including behavioral disorders such as ADHD. The Supreme Court also ruled that Supplemental Security Income (SSI) payments should include individuals with ADHD (so long as the ADHD is severe and the patient shows documented impairments in cognition or communication and social and personal functioning). Because, in part, of these incentives, by the mid-1990s, ADHD was becoming a much more popular diagnosis, with estimates that more than 5 percent of US children and adolescents had received diagnoses.

Within a few more years, millions of Americans were using the Internet to find information and could learn about ADHD in the privacy of their homes. Another important change in the late 1990s was the advent of enticing direct-to-consumer ads for ADHD medications (as well as many other medical and psychiatric pills) in magazines, on television, and via the Web. It's reasonable to assume that many parents, looking at the glossy photographs of cheerful children obediently doing their homework, were persuaded to take their irritable, distracted offspring in to see if they might qualify for a diagnosis.

As we'll explain in detail later, a critically important development that helped boost the national rates of ADHD came with state policies in the 1990s that made funding for schools dependent on a district's test scores. In 2001, President George W. Bush signed into law the federal No Child Left Behind Law, which extended this practice to those states that had not previously enacted such legislation.

Yet another reason for the rising rates of diagnoses is better reporting. At the turn of twenty-first century, the CDC first began tracking behavioral and neurodevelopmental conditions such as ADHD and autism-spectrum disorders. Questions were added to the National Survey of Children's Health, a large, periodic national survey of nearly 100,000 representative families throughout the United States. These questions included whether a doctor or other healthcare provider had ever told the parent that the child in question had been diagnosed with ADHD—and, if so, whether the child was being treated with medication.

The first survey including these questions was performed in 2003. At that time the overall percentage of youth aged 4–17 who had ever received a diagnosis was 7.8 percent. Four years later, in 2007, the percentage had jumped to 9.5 percent. By the third survey, in 2011–2012, the figure had risen again, to 11.0 percent: one in nine youth across this wide age span. As noted in the Introduction, this figure represents an increase of 41 percent in the 9-year period. Even more shocking, for boys who had reached adolescence, 20 percent had received a diagnosis—one in *five*.

These figures reflect parental reports of diagnoses, which are, as noted above, rates of *diagnosed* prevalence as opposed to true prevalence. Our educated guess is that despite some underdiagnosis (especially in girls), ADHD is now likely as a general rule to be overdiagnosed in many segments of the population, largely linked to cursory diagnostic procedures in many locales. Thus, we believe that the national diagnosed prevalence in the United States has by now outstripped the true prevalence.

As we highlight in later chapters, what's remarkable is not just the overall rise but the variation across states and regions. The South and Midwest regions of America have much higher rates of ADHD diagnosis than does the Pacific Coast region, creating an intriguing puzzle. At the same time, the rates of ADHD diagnosis have been rapidly rising in many parts of the developed world outside our borders. We address these questions later on in this chapter.

Do the Rising Rates of ADHD have Anything in Common with the Similarly Rising Rates of Autism?

In recent years, diagnoses of autism-spectrum disorders have been escalating at even faster rates than for ADHD. One immediate explanation is that rates of autism diagnosis have historically been quite low. They were still below one-tenth of 1 percent of the population of children and adolescents as recently as the early 1990s, when rates of ADHD were thought to be 3–5 percent of the population. With such initially low rates, any increases in assigning diagnoses naturally appears particularly large.

The rising rates of autism and ADHD do have a few things in common. One is that the official diagnostic criteria for both conditions have been loosened in recent years, making it easier to qualify for a diagnosis. Awareness of both conditions has also grown substantially. Another relatively recent change is that both diagnostic labels have enabled families to obtain services for their children. Policy changes governing both education and health insurance—for example, California now requires coverage of behavior therapy for autism—have made obtaining an autism diagnosis increasingly valuable, particularly if a child is struggling academically or socially.

There are also some reasons to suggest that the *true* prevalence (and not just the diagnoses) of these two disorders has grown. We elaborate on these in the next chapter, but they include increasing exposure to toxic chemicals and also an increasing number of babies surviving premature births and low birthweights. It is also possible, particularly in the case of ADHD, that the rapid increase in the numbers of young children in day care could explain some part of the increase in *diagnosed* prevalence, given the growing numbers of over-stressed children in such facilities and the greater numbers of teachers able to observe young children's behavior patterns in these settings.

Is this Disorder Something New or Has it Always Been Around in Some Form?

For millennia, doctors, philosophers, scientists, poets, and novelists have studied and commented on a variation of temperament that makes some people more impulsive, bold, and distracted than the rest of us. This variability has been variously interpreted as a physical defect, a moral failing, a family curse, or some ungainly combination of all three.

In ancient Greece, impulsive behavior was thought to be caused by an excess of red blood, treated with leeches. Yet it wasn't until the Age of Enlightenment, roughly 2,200 years later, that a Scottish physician, Sir Alexander Crichton, wrote about "morbid alterations of attention" characterized by extreme mental restlessness and distraction, which could become evident early in life or occur as the result of an illness, and which tended to sabotage a child's education.

Crichton described one feature of this condition as "the incapacity of attending with a necessary degree of constancy to any one object," which certainly sounds familiar as one of the diagnostic indicators of ADHD. He also wrote of an extreme state of reactivity to stimuli such as barking dogs or other sudden noises, a restlessness that patients with the condition called "the fidgets." Crichton went on to observe that the symptoms tended to diminish with age—as, centuries later, research showed they indeed do in as many as half of those with the disorder. Research has also confirmed that the most observable symptoms of overactivity tend to go underground by adolescence and beyond, whereas lack of organization and focus and mental restlessness are more likely to persist.

In the Victorian Age, through the mid-nineteenth century, the pioneering American psychologist William James built on Crichton's observations when he detailed his perspective on the links between attention, distraction, and immoral behavior—to the point of criminality—even as he doubted that much could be done to help people with problems in those domains.

Others disagreed, however, and over the course of the next several decades, the phenomenon we now know as ADHD took clearer shape, as a long line of doctors and scholars in Europe and the United States sought ways to help seriously distracted children. At the turn of the twentieth century, one of these pioneers, the British physician George Still, embarked on a groundbreaking series of lectures in which he defined the cluster of behaviors that today often accompany a diagnosis of ADHD. Still described a group of his young patients who shared what he called a major "defect in moral control." They were, as he said, not only inattentive but overactive, accident-prone, aggressive, defiant, sometimes cruel and dishonest, and strikingly insensitive to punishment.

In a soon-to-be classic portrait of a typical boy with the symptoms later known to belong to ADHD, the German physician Heinrich Hoffman wrote a bit of verse that was published in the medical journal *The Lancet* in 1904, describing naughty "Fidgety Phil," who:

> . . . won't sit still;
> He wriggles,
> And giggles,
> And then, I declare,
> Swings backwards and forwards,
> And tilts up his chair. . . .
> Till his chair falls over quite,
> Philip screams with all his might . . .

As George Still noted, the defiant behavior patterns he observed typically arose before the age of 8 and were more common in boys than in girls. They were also particularly common in families that included alcoholics and criminals—one of the first hints of a genetic explanation.

The search was on for a smoking gun. In the ensuing decades, investigators would seek clues to the roots of serious distraction with surveys, X-rays, EEGs, brain scans, clinical interviews, and genetic testing. Type in "attention deficit" today on PubMed, the leading Internet archive of medical journals and reports, and you'll find close to 30,000 papers published between 1966 and 2014, with more than two-thirds of these published between 2004 and 2014 alone.

Popular awareness of the powerful link between physical and mental health substantially increased for the first time in the World War I years, when the great encephalitis pandemic claimed at least 60 million lives throughout the world. Doctors were intrigued to find that many of the survivors experienced problems with attention and impulsivity. As they soon discovered, a pathogen was affecting the brain, in addition to other organs, and changing behavior. This first clear evidence linking biology and behavior was a precursor to our modern understanding of ADHD as linked to genes and prenatal influences, rather than upbringing or innate morality, a topic we more thoroughly discuss in the next chapter.

Reasoning backward, the early twentieth-century clinicians began to hypothesize that if these same behavior patterns were displayed in a given child or adolescent, there must be some underlying brain pathology—even if it were undetectable. This assumption led to the description of children with ADHD as suffering from "postencephalitic behavior disorder" and, later, "minimal brain damage," with the latter phrase subsequently softened to "minimal brain dysfunction" (MBD). These terms remained in common use in scientific literature and clinics for the next several decades.

By the 1950s, understanding of ADHD had developed sufficiently for scientists to become more precise in their language. Minimal brain dysfunction could encompass a long list of symptoms—including depression, delayed speech, and bed-wetting—that have little or nothing to do with the classic syndrome of distraction. Experts therefore tried out new phrases, such as "hyperkinetic impulse disorder"—and, in the late 1960s, "hyperkinetic reaction of childhood." "Hyperactivity" became the shorthand clinical label. In 1980, as we've explained, the term was further refined, to ADD.

As we'll elaborate later, it's intriguing to consider that the first major surge of interest and understanding of ADHD, along with more scrupulous identification of children who had the disorder, took place in the late nineteenth century, just as compulsory school was becoming the norm in developed nations. For the first time in history, the vast majority of children had to sit still and pay attention for sustained periods throughout a school day, taxing many of them beyond their capacity. It's a safe bet, therefore, that mandatory education was the first significant force that suggested the true prevalence of ADHD in children.

Focusing On: Prevalence

ADHD in some form has doubtless existed from the dawn of human history. Yet scientific and medical interest in it really took off at the dawn of compulsory mass education, beginning around the middle of the nineteenth century. There was something about kids having to sit in classrooms most of the day, behaving themselves and maintaining self-control, that made the extra-inattentive and extra-restless ones stand out. In fact, this was really the first time that outside observers—namely, teachers—got a chance to compare the behaviors of large groups of unrelated children. Today, approximately 11 percent of all US youth aged 4–17 have at some point received an ADHD diagnosis, according to the most recent available survey by the CDC, covering 2011–2012. This translates to approximately 6.4 million US children and adolescents. The estimates are less authoritative after age 17, but researchers believe that there may be around 10 million adults with the disorder in the United States.

3

WHAT CAUSES IT?

What is the Most Common Cause of ADHD?
(Spoiler Alert: It Runs in Families)

ADHD can be caused by one or more of several different factors that we'll list and explain in this chapter. But by far the single most common way to get it is from your ancestors. We know this from a large and still growing number of studies on twins and adopted children that have helped scientists disentangle the role of genes versus environments. Given that 100 percent heritability means that genes alone are responsible for differences between people with respect to a certain symptom, trait, or disorder, these studies have revealed that the basic symptoms of ADHD are approximately 75 percent heritable.

In other words, the main reason that some people are extremely attentive, some are completely distracted, and most are somewhere in the middle of the bell curve owes to genetic rather than environmental factors. This figure is lower than that for the heritability for height (which is about 90 percent) but more than for major depression (30–40 percent) and schizophrenia (60 percent), and nearly equal to the rate for bipolar disorder and autism (more than 80 percent), two of the psychiatric conditions with the highest genetic liability known to science.

Another way of conveying the genetic contribution to ADHD is as follows: among children with ADHD, 40 percent or more of their biological parents will also show significant symptoms, regardless of whether the parents have also been diagnosed. As we discuss in a later section of this chapter, this substantially adds to the difficulties that parents may have in managing offspring with ADHD, given that the parents themselves may be dealing with their own problems of disorganization and emotional overreactivity.

Heritability isn't a simple concept. Despite the high level of genetic influence involved in ADHD, there is no single gene that causes the disorder, as is also true for all other mental disorders and for nearly all complex physical diseases. As many as 50, 100, or more gene variations, or alleles, may contribute to ADHD by influencing the way the brain creates and responds to important chemical messengers associated with attention and motivation. We'll tell you more about these chemicals, known as neurotransmitters, later on, when we discuss what's going on in the brains of people with ADHD. But simply consider this landmark finding: scientists relatively recently discovered that a gene variation known as DRD4-7, commonly found in people diagnosed with ADHD, contributes to a lower rate of brain receptors for a key neurotransmitter called dopamine. The presence of this allele correlates with an unusual propensity to seek excitement and novelty, whereby people are prone to take risks that others typically avoid.

An important way to think about this is that if your brain does a poor job of processing dopamine, you're likely to be chronically sleepy-minded (the clinical term is "under-aroused")—fidgeting to stay alert or feeling a need to engage in high-risk behaviors to avoid the irritability and anxiety connected with boredom. This pattern helps explain why stimulant medications and therapies that aim to change behavior with a system of rewards can be successful in treating ADHD: They help supply some of the missing fuel for motivation.

Recent research has shown that some of the genes that raise the risk for ADHD are the same genes that raise the risk for autism, even though the two disorders manifest themselves quite differently. This intriguing finding shows us that there aren't necessarily specific genes for specific mental disorders but rather that certain genes sculpt the brain's development, which in turn is affected by other genes and by early environments to yield different kinds behavioral and emotional conditions.

We'll tell you more about such gene-environment interplay later on in this chapter, when we discuss the influence of parents and schools. For now, keep in mind that even for traits and behavior patterns with high heritability, changes in the environment over time can make such traits and behaviors more or less pronounced. Height is a good example. People today on average are several inches taller than their great-grandparents, but this is not because the genes for height have mutated over a few generations. Rather, changes in our diets over the last century have altered the influence of genes, or as scientists say, gene *expression*.

It may be the same with ADHD. Even though the disorder is highly heritable, relatively recent and quite dramatic changes in our modern environment—including the unrelenting flood of information from personal computers and cellphones and increasing societal pressures to multitask and perform ever faster and earlier—may be making most of us less attentive and more impulsive (and fast-tasking) than ever before. Still, genes make the key difference in determining which of us, in the midst of this changing information climate, will lie at the extremes of the curve. We like to put it this way: People with ADHD are our era's coal-mine canaries, more sensitive than most other individuals to shifting pressures for attention and achievement that may ultimately affect nearly everyone.

What Other Factors Might Cause ADHD?

Beyond genes, difficulties before or during birth, or during early childhood, can result in ADHD symptoms. Included

here is the exposure of a fetus to heavy metals, alcohol, nicotine, and toxic chemicals as well as other prenatal risks that
can lead to lower-than-normal birth weight. All of these can
contribute to the basic symptoms of inattention, impulsiveness, and, in some instances, hyperactivity.

Several studies have linked fetal or childhood exposure to
lead, even at very low levels, with cognitive and behavioral
deficits that resemble those of ADHD. Similarly, a pregnant
woman's excessive consumption of alcohol can produce what
are called fetal alcohol "effects," including classic ADHD
symptoms of inattention, impulsivity, hyperactivity, learning
problems, and sometimes aggression. (More extreme alcohol
consumption can cause fetal alcohol syndrome, with acute
damage to an infant's brain that may result in intellectual
disabilities as well as noticeable facial abnormalities.) There's
also evidence that a pregnant woman's smoking and even
second-hand smoke around a baby or child can lead to ADHD
symptoms.

In recent years, scientists have expressed concern about the
dangers to young brains stemming from even low-level exposure to toxic chemicals that have become increasingly common
in our environment. Chief among these is a class of organic
compounds known as organophosphates, which are used in
pesticides, fertilizers, herbicides, and solvents, with residue
left on much of our food. Although this field of study is still in
its infancy, researchers have found clear links between early
exposure to organophosphates and later symptoms of inattention and hyperactivity in addition to some symptoms of
autism.

Researchers have found similar links between ADHD-like
symptoms and exposure to phthalates and bisphenol A,
chemicals found in a wide range of everyday plastic products
including baby bottles, sippy cups, pacifiers, and teething
rings. Bisphenol A is used in hard plastic items, like the baby
bottles, whereas phthalates make plastic soft and flexible, for
items such as shower curtains, cosmetics, and many medical

devices. Both chemicals can leach from plastic into liquid and food, especially when items are heated or used for long periods of time. Both are also known to be endocrine disruptors, affecting thyroid functioning and hormones, with various harmful effects. The European Union has banned some of these chemicals, and some US industries are trying to end their use of them, but the US federal government has yet to step in, and the chemicals are so common that it could take many years for private efforts to replace them.

Another major concern is exposure to lead, as we've mentioned—for example, from the paint in homes built before 1978 or from leaded gasoline—and mercury, increasingly found in several species of fish. Both of these substances have been linked to brain damage including problems resembling ADHD. It's possible that children who begin life with certain genetic vulnerabilities may be extra-susceptible to the influence of such toxic chemicals, a pattern exemplifying *gene-environment interaction,* whereby the harm from an environmental exposure depends on the presence of a vulnerable genotype. Once again, it's clear that genes and environments are not separate in predisposing individuals to ADHD. Rather, they nearly always work together.

Moving down the list, being born prematurely, and especially at a lower-than-normal weight, is another risk factor for ADHD symptoms, as it also is for learning disorders, Tourette syndrome, and even cerebral palsy. Low-birthweight babies often suffer bleeding into brain regions associated with learning, motor behavior, and attention. Thanks to increasingly sophisticated neonatal intensive care, many more low-birthweight babies than ever before are now surviving. The unfortunate corollary is that this progress may be contributing, at least in part, to the rising rates of ADHD (not just diagnosed prevalence).

The moral of all these stories is to remind you that ADHD is a multifaceted syndrome with no single cause. Different developmental pathways may lead to the same basic symptoms. In some of the most severe cases, there may be combinations of genetic risk and exposure to the toxic substances noted above.

What's Going on Inside the Brains of People with ADHD that Causes the Symptoms?

Scientists have gathered evidence supporting several kinds of differences in the brains of people diagnosed with ADHD. You can think of them as belonging to one or more of three groups: chemical, structural, and functional. The bottom line is they're all biological, in contrast to the unfounded popular opinion that views ADHD as stemming from bad moral character and/or poor parenting.

Starting with the chemicals: The key word here is *dopamine*, a much-celebrated neurotransmitter underlying attention and motivation. Like other chemical messengers in the brain, dopamine carries electrical signals across synapses, the gaps between brain cells (neurons). Whenever this micro-transportation system flags, the brain can't function optimally.

Dopamine is one of a few different neurotransmitters implicated in ADHD. Another is norepinephrine, also known as noradrenaline, which plays a major role in impulse control. Dopamine, in contrast, is crucial for alertness, focus, and sensitivity to rewards. It might be thought of as the brain's elixir of excitement, awakening interest by drawing us to novelty (good or bad), such as a new sort of berry on a tree, a snake in the grass, or a check in the mail. Dopamine is the core neurotransmitter in only a few of the brain's major pathways, but these are directly relevant to motivation, effort, and self-regulation.

Too much dopamine can make you psychotic, while too little can literally immobilize you, as with the victims of Parkinson's disease. In recent years, scientists have learned that brains of people with ADHD have a major problem with this vital chemical. They either make too little of it, have fewer receptors for it, or use it less efficiently. Nora Volkow's brain-scan-based research at the National Institute on Drug Abuse has documented that the brains of carefully diagnosed adults with ADHD contain significantly fewer receptors for dopamine in precisely those neural pathways relevant for registering reward or maintaining focus and attention. Volkow found this to be true even though the subjects had never taken medication, which means that the findings can't be attributed to any stimulant-related effects on dopamine receptors. Her conclusion, shared by other leading experts in the field today, is that for at least some individuals with ADHD, there's an inborn dopamine deficiency.

Moving on to larger-scale structural differences, developmental neuroscientists have made some startling recent discoveries, including that important brain structures in people with ADHD are on average smaller than those of their counterparts.

Over the course of several years, Philip Shaw and his team at the National Institute of Mental Health have performed a series of periodic brain scans of children with ADHD and a control group. The scans focused in particular on the cortex—the brain's outermost layer, densely packed with neurons—and even more specifically the part of the cortex covering the frontal lobes. Lying just behind the forehead and toward the top of the head, the frontal lobes are known to play a major role in self-control and a host of executive functions.

During normal development, the frontal cortex reaches a maximum thickness at around age 6. But in the sample of over 200 children with ADHD, the maximum was not achieved until age 9 or later, signaling a 3-year developmental gap in the brains of children with clear attention deficits and impulsivity. Even after childhood, the brains of the diagnosed youth continued to lag behind those of the control group during adolescence, when the cortex typically thins. Shaw and his team also found a link between the degree of cortical thickening and the severity of ADHD symptoms in the diagnosed sample.

In light of these findings, it shouldn't be so surprising that many 11-year-olds with ADHD behave more like 8-year-olds. Decades ago, clinicians often referred to children with ADHD symptoms as being immature. The new science proves them right, in a sense: They have slower-maturing brains.

Do the brains of people with ADHD ever catch up to those of their peers? At this writing that question remains unanswered. Some brain-scan studies suggest that on average the overall brain volume of people with ADHD, both children and adults, is somewhat lower than in typically developing individuals.

Added to chemical and structural differences that can lead to ADHD symptoms are the functional, or dynamic ones. Functional magnetic resonance imaging (fMRI) analyzes patterns of blood flow, revealing which parts of the brain are being activated during performance of various cognitive tasks. Many investigations using this technology have shown that activation patterns in pathways between the frontal lobes and deeper structures involved in learning and self-regulation are particularly inefficient in individuals with ADHD when the participants are engaged in tests of working memory, attention, or other aspects of cognition. It's as though the brains of people with ADHD don't function as smoothly or efficiently as those of normally developing individuals.

Another kind of research takes a different tack, analyzing the brain's tendencies when individuals are at rest or just daydreaming. Intriguingly, the brain shows distinct patterns of activation and organization during such down time. It now appears that this "resting state" brain activity of people with ADHD intrudes on their task performance when attention and concentration are really needed. In other words, there's now neural evidence that people with ADHD may need to work extra hard to prevent an underaroused brain from taking over when focused work is required.

How Much Influence Do Parents Have, if Any—And in What Ways?

Throughout this book, we hope to impress on you that ADHD symptoms, along with most if not all other human behaviors, arise and take shape due to a combination of nature and nurture, biology and environment, innate traits and changing context. All of these dynamics mold a person's personality and behavior throughout a lifetime, creating vicious or virtuous circles. Another spoiler alert: Although ADHD always begins with biology, a parent's behavior can matter quite a bit.

In 1998, Judith Rich Harris published a much-discussed book entitled *The Nurture Assumption: Why Children Turn Out the Way They Do*. Most controversially, she argued that parents have little significant impact on their children and that genes and peers far outweigh them in influence. Some of her arguments are in fact worthwhile. Developmental psychology during much of the twentieth century overattributed childhood behavior to the influence of parents. Yet considerable evidence suggests that Harris's main claim is greatly exaggerated. Parents and other caretakers indisputably matter a lot and in some key ways that we are only beginning to fathom.

Consider the extreme example of the children born in Eastern European orphanages during the 1980s, many of whom, due to horrific neglect, grew up deprived of all but minimal social contact. They ended up, not surprisingly, with serious problems in relating to others as well as with severely compromised cognitive and language ability. Many also had ADHD-like symptoms including acute difficulties with sustaining attention and self-control. In other words, beyond the usual genetic and biological risks, an extremely deprived social environment appears to be one of the many triggers for ADHD behavior.

It's important not to read too much into this rare case. It's a common misperception that what psychologists call insecure attachment, which refers to babies' patterns of failing to form a secure bond with caregivers, causes ADHD. Problems with attachment do often result in aggression and sometimes depression, but not in ADHD symptoms per se, except, as noted, in cases of utter deprivation. Thus, the isolated example of the Eastern European orphans does little to bolster the popular but wrong belief that bad parenting causes ADHD.

At the same time, it's certainly true that skillful parenting can make a great difference in the lives of children with biological risk for ADHD. Researchers have found the gold standard to be "authoritative" parenting, which blends warmth with clear limits and strong guidance toward independence. (A style encompassing too many limits and too little warmth is branded "authoritarian" parenting, while warmth without clear limits is "permissive.") The value of a parent's love can't be discounted when considering a child's mental health. One study of twins with low birthweights found a direct correlation between a mother's affectionate behavior toward her babies and the later development of ADHD symptoms: Greater warmth was associated with lower symptom levels. This finding appears to offer further confirmation of a classic 2004 study on rats, in which McGill University scientist Michael Meany found that the degree to which a mother rat licks and grooms her pups will determine whether certain genes in the pups' brains are turned on or off. As adults, the better-nurtured rats appear to be less fearful and release less of the stress hormone cortisol when startled. Surely, the behavior of both human mothers and fathers toward their babies, children, and teens has many impacts we are only beginning to understand.

Hinshaw's own research has found that boys with ADHD whose primary caregivers deployed high levels of authoritative parenting, that skillful combo of warmth and limits that the ADHD expert Edward Hallowell calls "super-parenting," showed the highest levels of social competence during summer camp programs. Testing a similar hypothesis, the prominent psychologist Michael Posner, at the University of Oregon, has shown that cold, dictatorial, "authoritarian" parents increase the odds that children born with the DRD4-7 allele, the gene variation linked to risk-taking, will develop a difficult temperament, possibly combined with problems in executive functions. Once again, this result and others like it suggest that certain genes may become activated (or "expressed") only or mostly within certain environments—demonstrating the complex ways in which genes and environments are closely intertwined.

To cite just one more example of this general rule, Susan Campbell of the University of Pittsburgh carefully assessed preschool children with early signs of ADHD as rated by parents and preschool teachers and found that parents who responded with negativity and harshness to their children's behavior tended to exacerbate their children's symptoms—not only right away but over many years. It's worth emphasizing that the parents didn't create those symptoms, the origins of which were undoubtedly related to genes and temperament, but appeared to be pouring gas on a developing fire.

It's now time to introduce a bit more complexity. Consider the fact that a child born to be impulsive—to run around the grocery store, knock things over, drop an iPhone in the toilet, pull the cat's tail, steal a sibling's diary, and inspire weekly if not daily irate calls from his or her school—is not an easy child to raise. What makes all of that exponentially harder, and a sure-fire recipe for family chaos, is that, given the strongly hereditary nature of ADHD, one or both of that child's parents may be struggling with the same disorder or at least with many similar symptoms. People with ADHD, adults and children alike, are often so impulsive that they unintentionally violate others' personal boundaries, betray confidences, and react emotionally. None of these actions is conducive to calm parenting or domestic peace. Moreover, a parent distracted and frazzled by unpaid bills, unmet deadlines, and an unclean kitchen is not mentally well equipped to provide authoritative parenting. Such parents tend to struggle and fail to remain calm and set clear, firm limits, resulting in the worsening of their children's behavior. Seriously distracted parents may also not be the best medical advocates for their kids, given that this task usually requires wending one's way through a complicated medical system and making sure the children regularly take whatever medications are prescribed.

In short, it's important to keep in mind that children influence their parents as much as (or even more than) vice versa. Psychologists once assumed, for instance, that intrusive, controlling mothers were making their children hyperactive. Then scientists found that when those kids with ADHD took stimulants, improving their behavior, the moms nagged less. The nagging, in other words, was a reaction to and not a cause of the children's behavior. (On the other hand, the child's medication did not substantially increase the parents' use of more positive practices, suggesting strongly that additional treatment in behavior management should complement medication, as we address in Chapter 8.)

In another illuminating study, researchers went so far as to temporarily switch mothers of children with aggressive conduct disorder with mothers of more typical kids. In no time, the previously calm moms of the "normal" youth were pestering and criticizing, at the same time that the original naggers had calmed down. Moreover, in recent research from England, performed with adoptive families—that is, in which parents and children do not share genes—it was found that children with ADHD symptoms provoked hostile parenting, and that in turn, such hostile treatment increased the risk and severity of later ADHD-related symptoms. It's all more evidence that beyond the role of biology in explaining ADHD, parent-child interaction and reciprocal influences are also very much at play.

The common pattern is that a young child with a difficult temperament can frustrate an otherwise mild-mannered adult, leading to emotional reactions from the parent that, in turn, lead to worse behavior from the child. And, in the case of ADHD, such difficult temperament can appear even in the first year or two of life, setting off a chain of reactions and counterreactions that can last a lifetime. The child's extraordinary resistance and defiance may lead the parent either to back off entirely or to resort to harsh punishment—or sometimes both, in alternating cycles—making the child even more angry and aggressive.

If left unaddressed, these effects can play off each other and multiply. For instance, the rebellious child's teachers and friends may increasingly brand him or her as a troublemaker, reinforcing the kid's worst instincts. Such potentially escalating risks make it all the more important for parents of children with ADHD to make sure they acknowledge and treat any mental and emotional problems of their own that may be compromising their ability to help their offspring.

What Role Do Schools and Academic Pressures Play in Today's High Rates of ADHD?

One of our mantras is that ADHD, along with other variabilities of behavior, is a condition that stems both from individuals and the contexts surrounding them. It's particularly striking to consider that the earliest clinical accounts of behaviors linked to ADHD coincided with the advent of compulsory education in the Western world. In the United States, beginning in the second half of the nineteenth century, the majority of the nation's children for the first time had to participate daily in classrooms, sit still for hours at a time, and do things that human brains had never evolved to do until that point, such as learn to read (reading is a relatively recent addition to the human repertoire, dating back only a few thousand years—and for most of that period, only for children of the elite).

The early "common schools" of the nineteenth and early twentieth centuries were designed to resemble factories, in which children were the passive recipients of a rigid curriculum. Conformity, organization, and tolerance for rote memorization became prized behaviors, as they continue to be in many of today's public schools, particularly as teachers are besieged by pressures to teach to standardized tests. What's more, then, as well as now, the expectation has been that children in grades K–12 will become competent generalists. The problem is that such environments can be downright hellish for children who struggle with sustaining attention and self-control, and who do best when they are able to discover a niche of learning that holds their attention. Easily bored, to the point of painful anxiety and, all too often, misbehavior, they are routinely labeled as "bad kids," both punished and rejected.

Making matters still worse has been the steady average national decline in available time for recess, lunch, physical education, and art and music classes, mostly due to budget shortfalls and pressure on teachers to prepare students for standardized tests. There's a lot less time for kids to get out of their chairs, move around, and refresh their brains, which, naturally, is hardest on kids whose brains are underaroused from the start.

Given all this, it probably shouldn't be surprising that one-third or more of US children with ADHD drop out of high school, often sabotaging their chances for well-paid and interesting jobs. Life may get easier in college, if they manage to get there, given the greater freedom to choose classes and schedules. Nonetheless, the challenges of college life are acute for many students with ADHD. Many college students have trouble organizing their lives independently for the first time, but those with ADHD can truly flounder, particularly when lacking special support.

What Do People with ADHD Need to Know about Video Games, Social Media, and Other Forms of Screen Entertainment?

Video games offer players intense, often relentless action, dramatic stories, the thrill of competition, constant rewards, and feedback tailored directly to recent performance—in other words, precisely the types of stimuli that the ADHD brain craves and rarely gets in mundane everyday life.

Parents of ADHD gamers reasonably worry when their kids start demanding to spend hour after hour in front of a screen. Our strong advice is to not waste time worrying but instead to take firm action, limiting screen time from an early age. Your child doesn't need to have a TV set or Xbox in his or her room, or unlimited use of a smartphone by the time he or she gets to middle school. Such choices, in fact, can do considerable damage.

For many children, video games, television, and other forms of screen time become so enticing that they can easily interfere with social life, school, or work. In fact, some research has found that dopamine levels at least double when people play rewarding video games. Because kids with ADHD are so much more drawn to these rewarding distractions, they're at special risk of losing out on important experiences, including friendships, sports, music, and job experience. Furthermore, some researchers have found evidence that although the surfeit of screen time doesn't cause ADHD, it *can* aggravate the symptoms. A team of researchers at Iowa State University who surveyed 1,323 children aged 8 to 11, and 210 young adults, mostly between 18 and 24, found that attention problems increased as did the number of hours playing video games. The same was true for hours watching TV. In fact, children who exceeded the 2 hours of daily screen time recommended by the American Academy of Pediatrics were more likely to have attention problems.

Young children are particularly vulnerable. In 2011, researchers measured the performance of 4-year-olds on cognitive tasks after showing some of them 9-minute clips of a fast-paced cartoon from *SpongeBob SquarePants*. Other children either watched a slower-paced show or didn't watch TV at all. As it turned out, the children who watched the fast-paced cartoon were more impatient and had more trouble following directions, revealing a temporary dip in their executive functions.

The trouble with this and other studies showing similar links is that researchers so far haven't been able to answer the real-world, chicken-and-egg question of whether the symptoms of ADHD lead to more screen time or more screen time leads to higher levels of ADHD. In either case, however, it's not great news for screen devotees.

Some research strongly suggests that overindulging in video games is a predominantly male problem. Psychologist Anatol Tolchinsky at Eastern Michigan University performed a study of 216 college students, both men and women, who had ADHD symptoms ranging from mild to severe and who played video games at least once a week. Researchers found that the men had higher rates of "problematic" screen time (i.e., time devoted to games interfered with hygiene, sleep, school, and relationships) than the women. The main problem in these cases seemed to be the young men's poor time management skills. Some of the subjects simply didn't realize how many hours they had spent on the games. Women in the study not only reported fewer game-related problems but logged half as many hours per week playing the games as their male classmates.

A widespread concern among parents of children both with and without ADHD is the content of the electronic behavior, particularly the violent nature of such explicit videogames as "Grand Theft Auto" or "Call of Duty." In 1974, when screen violence was a faint shadow of what it is today, the consensus (including a unanimous Scientific Advisory Committee report) indicated that televised violence has an adverse effect. Ever since then, however, opposing sides have warred over this issue. Those who think the concerns are exaggerated have contended that in the same years that violence in the media has increased, rates of male violence throughout America have steadily declined, strongly suggesting that media exposure can't be causing the aggressive behavior. In 1999, the federal government backed away from its earlier statement, citing problems with the research.

More recent studies, however, have offered more support to those who worry over the impact of violent media. Although one major study in 2010 found that neither video game violence nor TV violence predicted serious acts of youth aggression or violence, particularly including the series of school shootings that have horrified the nation, systematic, careful reviews of the accumulated evidence have indeed linked random exposure of youth to violent as opposed to nonviolent media with short-term increases in aggressive behavior and decreases in empathy and helpful behavior. Furthermore, longitudinal studies have shown that children with initially high aggression are attracted to more violent forms of media, and that this exposure appears to increase their initial propensity for violence.

Returning to the issue of screen-time and ADHD symptoms, one certain cause for concern is the impact of electronic media on sleep. In June of 2012, the American Medical Association warned that exposure to excessive light at night, including light emitted by screens, "can disrupt sleep or exacerbate sleep disorders, especially in children and adolescents." Although any light at night can be disruptive, the "blue light" produced from smartphones and computers is particularly harmful in this regard, as it has been shown to suppress melatonin, a hormone that helps regulate sleep. Again, parents of children with ADHD, who already may be having trouble sleeping, should have firm rules about electronics in the bedroom or risk having symptoms worsened by a sleep disorder. We'll talk more about the link between poor sleep and ADHD in Chapter 4.

Focusing On: Causes

ADHD is more often than not the result of genes, but the story doesn't end there. Exposure to toxic substances, including lead, mercury, pesticides, plastic additives, alcohol, and tobacco, can create or aggravate ADHD-like symptoms. The symptoms arise due to brain dynamics that can include problems with important neurochemicals, primarily dopamine and norepinephrine, that help maintain alertness, sustained attention, and impulse control. The brains of children with ADHD are also structurally and dynamically different from those of their peers, specifically including delays in maturation of the frontal cortex. ADHD is primarily a problem of biology, but context is also crucial. The behavior of parents and other caretakers can make a big difference in the emergence and severity of symptoms, as researchers have found, and the behavior of children with ADHD will vary greatly depending on whether they are bored or challenged, making school environments hugely influential as well. Finally, ADHD is not caused by excessive time exposed to computers, TV, and smartphones, but there are indications that overdoing "screen time" can disrupt sleep, which may worsen symptoms, and also, if the content is violent, spark aggression.

4

HOW DO YOU KNOW IF
YOU HAVE IT?

*Under What Circumstances Should Your Child, Your Partner—Or
You Yourself—Be Evaluated for ADHD?*

Many core ADHD symptoms, particularly hyperactivity and impulsivity, first appear during the preschool years. Yet except in extreme cases, when the child is at risk of being expelled or is physically dangerous, it's usually not until grade school that ADHD symptoms will lead to assessment and treatment. Most often, a parent will consider bringing the child for an evaluation after one or more teachers has complained about classroom problems such as tuning out, acting up, or failing to work up to the youth's potential. For children with the purely inattentive variety of ADHD, problems can take longer to emerge but typically show up by middle school, when demands on students substantially increase, requiring more sustained focus and organization as well as the ability to keep track of multiple teachers in a changing daily schedule. For adults with ADHD symptoms, the impetus to seek a diagnosis may come from a loved one, spouse, or employer who values the relationship but is frustrated by behavior that can include poor listening skills, chronic lateness, messiness, failure to keep up with bills and household chores, emotional reactivity, and general unreliability. When additional disorders (e.g., substance abuse, aggressive behavior, and impairing anxiety) emerge, it's obviously even more important to seek help.

All symptoms of ADHD may be common in the general population on an occasional basis and especially during or after a stressful event. It's the frequency, intensity, duration, and impairing nature of such behaviors that tip the scales toward considering a formal evaluation. Along the way, it's a good idea for the parents of children who may have ADHD—or the adult and his or her partners—to talk with other experienced families or individuals, to attend meetings of support groups, and to educate themselves as much as possible.

Who is Most Likely to Diagnose ADHD?

All licensed physicians and mental health professionals are technically qualified to diagnose ADHD. Currently, the majority of US children are diagnosed by their pediatricians, which we consider a discouraging state of affairs, given that most pediatricians aren't sufficiently trained in mental illness in general and ADHD in particular. Moreover, although pediatricians are authorized to prescribe medication, and many do, few are expert in calculating optimal dosage levels and monitoring effectiveness—and even fewer are well-informed about behavioral, school, and family-based interventions. Many pediatricians are aware of these limitations but end up conducting evaluations anyway, due to the serious national shortage of child and adolescent psychiatrists and developmental-behavioral pediatricians—professionals who have received specific training in behavioral and emotional problems of youth. On the other hand, clinical child psychologists can be a good option for diagnosis; they outnumber child and adolescent psychiatrists and developmental-behavioral pediatricians and, if well trained, can offer a wide range of psychosocial treatments following a thorough evaluation.

Adults may be more likely to turn to a specialist, such as a psychologist or psychiatrist with expertise in ADHD. Yet many adults also rely on their general practitioners, who can provide prescriptions for ADHD medication—but all too often, again, without specialty training or the time to provide a careful diagnostic workup.

How Should ADHD be Diagnosed?

Although the precise numbers are not known, the unfortunate reality is that too many evaluations of people suspected of having ADHD take place in a clinical appointment lasting fewer than 10 or 15 minutes. In such cases, a doctor—usually a pediatrician or internist—might ask general questions and listen to family complaints, perhaps even going through a list of ADHD symptoms in cursory fashion. Such a doctor may diagnose someone with ADHD and prescribe medication then and there. Yet this is hardly the gold standard for an accurate diagnosis, in which it's essential to obtain information from others affected by the patient's behavior, such as a child's teacher or an adult's significant other. Experienced clinicians understand that ADHD-related problems don't readily show up in a one-on-one interview or testing situation; rather, they reveal themselves most strongly in everyday behavior displayed in the real world. Moreover, people with ADHD are often inadequate witnesses of their own behavior, and may also be in denial.

The official diagnostic guide, called the *Diagnostic and Statistical Manual of Mental Disorders*, or DSM, says a clinician should conclude that someone has ADHD only if the problems have been present from an early age (typically emerging before age 12), are chronic (even though their severity can fluctuate from day to day), are cross-situational (in other words, present in at least two important settings, such as home and school or home and the workplace) and are impairing (such that academics, relationships, job performance, and judgment are compromised).

The DSM lists a total of 18 symptoms of ADHD, with nine each pertaining to the inattentive and hyperactive forms. For children and youth up through 16 years of age, six of the nine symptoms of either of these presentations are required for a diagnosis. After age 17, only five of the nine symptoms within each domain are necessary.

A thorough clinician will provide parents and patients with checklists of symptoms, seeking to collect more than one impression of the individual's problems in different contexts. For children, parents and teachers should fill out the forms, while for adults, partners and employers are ideal as an addition to the adult patient's own self-reporting. The best checklists allow the diagnostician to compare symptom levels with those of other people of the same age as the individual in question.

Some lists are limited to the 18 ADHD symptoms spelled out in the DSM, but many clinicians use broader checklists that include questions about anxiety, depression, aggression, and possibly also autistic symptoms. These lengthier scales are particularly helpful for an initial evaluation, as they help rule out other conditions that might resemble ADHD and also bring to light potential accompanying problems. As we explain later in this chapter, it's also important to rule out issues such as sleep disorders or thyroid dysfunction before assuming someone has an attention disorder.

Respondents are typically asked to rate each item on a 3- or 4-point scale (with zero signifying "not at all," 1 "just a little," 2 "pretty much," and 3 "very much"). Scores of 2 or 3 are typically counted as a "yes" for the presence of the symptom.

For evaluations of children, some especially conscientious doctors will seek ratings from former teachers as well as the current teacher in order to ascertain patterns of behavior across the years. A child may well behave much differently depending on his or her relationship with a particular teacher. A review of report cards and school records (or for adults, job evaluations) can yield important information, not only about the precise numbers of symptoms but about the kinds of academic or work situations that are most likely to lead to problems. Even more helpful—although typically rare, due to time and cost considerations—are interviews with the teachers and observations of a child's behavior during the school day. It could be the case, for example, that in a particularly disorganized classroom, nearly every student is exhibiting ADHD symptoms. In another instance, it may be the transitions from one activity to another or from indoor to outdoor time that serve as the catalysts for the relevant problems. For inattentive youth, parents may not see the academic problems their child is experiencing as readily as teachers (except, perhaps, during homework).

A high-quality evaluation will include time for the examiner to conduct a detailed review of the patient's medical and psychological history. This includes a long interview with a patient, parent, and ideally someone else closely related to the patient to construct what's known as a *developmental history*. Such information is needed to understand possibly influential events during the person's infancy, toddlerhood, and preschool years. These may include neglect or abuse, a family's frequent moves, medical problems, accidents, and/or delays in speech, language, and motor skills. When it comes to adults, it's also important to determine when the ADHD symptoms began, given that the symptoms typically emerge in childhood.

We imagine that at this point you may be shaking your head in disbelief, wondering what kind of doctor or therapist would ever have this kind of time. Unfortunately, we concur. Most children and adults receiving ADHD diagnoses today are getting them after extremely brief examinations, which, as we've noted, explains some of the current patterns of overdiagnosis and overmedication. We are describing an ideal, although at minimum we do believe that several hours of a clinician's time, including collecting and scoring rating scales, obtaining a detailed family and developmental history, engaging in discussion with teachers (or employers), and writing a detailed report is needed to ensure accuracy. In complex cases (e.g., for those with significant anxiety or aggression), even more time may be required. When significant learning problems are involved, additional cognitive and achievement testing may also be in order, as discussed later in this chapter. How far from the norm must the symptoms be to make a diagnosis?

Just as with inches of height, points of blood pressure, or the cardinal features of depression, ADHD symptoms exist on a continuum. There is no magic place on this bell curve where the normal range stops and the atypical part of the spectrum begins. The DSM offers guidelines—namely, that the symptoms must have impaired the person in two or more settings for at least 6 months—suggesting that what's most important is the impairment and not just the number of symptoms. Researchers have found that when a person's ADHD symptoms are extreme (i.e., in the upper 5 or even 7 percent of the curve), he or she is likely to be impaired both academically and socially and needs a diagnosis. Even so, it's always important to consider the context. A 7-foot-tall basketball player may be graceful on the court but awkward getting into a taxi. A doctor with a restless, anxious temperament may feel comfortable in an emergency room but nowhere else. Again, it's not just the severity of the problems but how they influence the individual's performance in crucial aspects of life. How far from the norm must the symptoms be to make a diagnosis?

Why Do the Symptoms Show Up More Often in School and on the Job than at Other Times?

We've already explained that ADHD is a disorder not just of attention span and distractibility but of motivation, the latter encompassing the capacity to be interested in routine tasks or ones that place high demands on organization and focus. Because so many people with ADHD have a problem with processing dopamine, the neurotransmitter governing our relationship to rewards, they can seem to slack off without frequent enticements. When work or school becomes routine or particularly challenging, or when someone else (e.g., a teacher or boss) is calling the shots, people with ADHD often start fidgeting and daydreaming. Yet when such people are intrinsically interested in an activity—be it a march to protest climate change or a few hours playing Grand Theft Auto—the rules change. Controversies are particularly enticing for many people with ADHD, who are drawn to strong emotions. So are video games, with their strong reward systems in the form of noise, flashing lights, and accumulating points. Yet just because people with ADHD are unusually drawn to video games doesn't mean you should assume they will be naturally skilled at them. The Canadian investigator Rosemary Tannock has shown that youth with ADHD actually perform worse than control subjects on those games, despite their seeming to be extrafocused. The same information-processing issues that plague schoolwork are also apparent in this realm.

Is There Any Objective Assessment for ADHD, Such as a Blood Test or Brain Scan?

The short answers are no and no. For years scientists have been hotly pursuing a so-called biomarker for ADHD that would be free of subjective influence, such as measurements of chemicals in the bloodstream, performance on computerized attention tasks, or highly detailed pictures from brain scans. But they haven't found one yet that clearly indicates which individuals do or do not have ADHD.

There are some small signs of progress. In 2013, the US Food and Drug Administration (FDA) approved a test for ADHD that measures brain waves—the electrical impulses produced by clusters of neurons—via an electroencephalogram (EEG) that uses electrodes attached to a person's scalp. There is persuasive evidence that a dominant pattern of slow-frequency theta and beta waves may serve as a partial marker for ADHD. Another recent FDA-approved ADHD diagnostic tool is a computerized test of sustained attention and impulse control that features an infrared tracking device to detect subtle head and body movements during the testing. This test was invented by Dr. Martin Teicher, a psychiatrist based at the prestigious McLean Hospital in Belmont, Massachusetts, and some insurance companies are now reimbursing clinicians who employ it. In our opinion, however, although both of the tests may indeed add to a clinician's information and improve the accuracy of diagnoses, neither can serve as worthy substitutes for the kind of thorough assessment we've described. In both cases, the devices measure behavior in only one setting, and for a limited time. They can't replicate constantly changing, real-world environments such as classrooms and offices.

On the outer bounds of credibility are entrepreneurs who tell you that they can diagnose your ADHD with a single brain scan. We'll address this development in more detail in Chapter 10, but in short: Don't believe them.

What Do You Need to Know about the Diagnostic and Statistical Manual (DSM)?

The DSM is America's most universally used and trusted guide on how to diagnose mental illness, but it is also one of the most controversial books ever written.

Published and periodically updated by the American Psychiatric Association, the DSM is a comprehensive volume that describes hundreds of mental disorders. Now in its fifth edition, it has become indispensable for America's clinicians, researchers, pharmaceutical firms, drug-regulation agencies, health insurance companies, the legal system, and policymakers. The first, extremely slender edition of the DSM was published in 1952, when it was more of a collection of statistics than a comprehensive guide to diagnoses. In that manual, there were precisely two disorders recognized as beginning in childhood. In contrast, the current, fifth edition (known as

DSM-5) published in 2013, contains scores of mental disorders with origins in the early years of life.

Clearly, the domain of mental illness has expanded greatly over the last six decades, given increased scientific investigation of the brain and behavior, vastly enhanced clinical interest, and—some would contend—greatly increased tendencies to medicalize all too many kinds of behavior. In other words, it can be tempting to label normal variations in behavior and even developmentally appropriate traits as "pathology." Along these lines, the DSM has generated increasing controversy in recent years. Critics have argued that its definitions are both too rigid—arbitrarily branding behavior as either normal or disturbed—and too subjective. To be sure, critiques have been aimed at other efforts at standards for conditions (such as high cholesterol levels) that fall on a continuum. But mental conditions without unequivocal biomarkers are more contentious and indeed more subject to bias. Parents who rate their child's ADHD symptoms, for example, may be influenced by their own degree of stress, depression, or attitudes toward the child.

Another important critique aims at potential financial conflicts of interest among the psychiatrists who help write the rules. Many of these authors serve on boards or speakers' bureaus of pharmaceutical firms, or receive grants from them for their research. In fact, in 2006, the *Washington Post* reported that every single expert involved in writing criteria for the DSM had ties to companies selling drugs for the relevant ailments. The obvious danger is that they may make diagnostic guidelines too loose, expanding the potential field of people who are eligible—and with that, the market for sales of medication.

The DSM is used mainly in the United States. A more comprehensive competitor, the World Health Organization's *International Classification of Diseases* (ICD), which includes both mental and physical disorders, is used by most of the rest of the world, sometimes in conjunction with the DSM. The ICD refers to what we know of as ADHD as hyperkinetic disorder (HKD), and its guidelines are somewhat tighter, requiring, for example, that symptoms emerge by age 6 rather than by age 12. There is also no purely inattentive form of HKD.

Guidebooks such as the DSM serve many purposes. They present the most up-to-date scientific knowledge about disorders, help assure that clinicians use the same standards, and provide the basis for insurance coverage. Yet experienced clinicians refrain from taking them too literally, leaving room for nuances and exceptions. And the categories within the DSM don't always map onto the complicated developmental pathways that lead to symptom display.

What is Neuropsychological Testing, and is it Ever a Good Idea?

Neuropsychological testing refers to an extensive battery of tests related to cognition, attention, executive functions, IQ, and even emotional well-being. The procedure has grown in popularity in recent years, given society's increasing awareness of the complex variety of childhood and adult mental health issues and the clamor for enhanced understanding as to why some individuals aren't learning or functioning up to their potential. The battery of tests can yield detailed information about strengths and weaknesses (e.g., stronger verbal than nonverbal abilities, particular problems with working memory, issues with visual versus auditory processing), providing recommendations for treatment and potentially for school accommodations.

It's not cheap: Testing can cost as much as $300 an hour, with 20 or more hours needed for evaluations and for writing up results. Some clinicians charge as much as $10,000 for a complete workup. If the child is having serious problems at school, it is sometimes possible to get the school psychologist to do at least some of these tests, as part of an individual educational program (as discussed later; see Chapter 9).

The advantage of the tests is that they provide a detailed map of someone's mental performance, rather than a single diagnosis. It can often be advantageous for parents to share such reports with a child's teachers, who may have misinterpreted the youth's behavior as rebellious, stubborn, or the product of daydreaming when in fact the child is struggling with a processing deficit and/or poor working memory.

Intelligence quotient (IQ) tests themselves provide a neuropsychological profile across their many subtests, along with the overall IQ score that purports to measure the individual's intellectual potential. Reading and math tests yield a clear picture of academic problems. Such tests can establish the presence of learning disorders, but they do not rule in or rule out ADHD on their own.

In sum, neuropsychological tests of various processing abilities can be, in some cases, a useful supplement, but they do not replace the careful evaluation of the individual's behavior in real-world, day-to-day settings, necessary for establishing a diagnosis of ADHD.

What Kinds of Professional Guidelines Exist for the Diagnosis of ADHD?

Two major professional organizations, the American Academy of Child and Adolescent Psychiatry and the American Academy of Pediatrics, maintain detailed guidelines for diagnosing ADHD, based on the gold-standard, evidence-based practices we've described in this chapter. The problem is that only a minority of professionals follow them, and no governing body enforces them. Unfortunately, as well, few if any insurance plans reimburse for the time and effort required to follow such authoritative guidelines.

Most general practitioners and pediatricians are not well trained in the procedures needed to diagnose ADHD, nor, as we've mentioned, do even conscientious and informed clinicians usually have the time and budget to follow them. This state of affairs sadly continues, even as evidence accumulates of the extravagant long-term costs of quick-and-dirty evaluations both in terms of personal suffering and financially—with taxpayers shelling out hundreds of billions of dollars a year for costs of untreated ADHD.

What Kinds of Problems or Conditions Produce Symptoms Similar to ADHD, and How Can Clinicians Distinguish Which Issue or Issues to Treat First?

Several physical and mental problems can produce symptoms resembling those of ADHD, such as inattention, distraction, disorganization, and forgetfulness, which at least sometimes need to be treated in a different manner. A good clinician must be able to identify and assess them before deciding that someone's primary problem is ADHD. The technique for doing this is known as *differential diagnosis*, referring to a process of elimination by gathering evidence including a patient's medical history and symptoms.

Emotional and behavioral problems that can produce symptoms similar to those of ADHD include the following:

- **Anxiety disorders**: These include generalized anxiety disorder, in which someone worries constantly about almost everything; obsessive-compulsive disorder (OCD), characterized by recurrent, unwanted, intrusive thoughts (obsessions) and a compulsive need to perform repetitive actions to undo these thoughts (compulsions); specific phobias (such as fear of heights or social encounters); and post-traumatic stress disorder (PTSD), which can emerge in the wake of physical or sexual abuse as well as other traumatic life experiences. All of these disorders can understandably diminish concentration but often exist independent of ADHD. For example, although ADHD symptoms are unrelenting, symptoms related to anxiety are typically intermittent, and tied to particular triggering stimuli. The exception here is generalized anxiety disorder, in which the individual is fearful of most aspects of everyday life.

Whereas some anxiety symptoms, including distraction and forgetfulness, may appear to be similar to symptoms of ADHD, they require significantly different treatment. Stimulants, for instance, may well make a person with a primary anxiety disorder even more anxious. All this helps explain why it's so important for a competent clinician to ask the patient, and, if possible, other informants, detailed questions about his or her symptoms.

- **Mood disorders—primarily including depression and bipolar disorder:** Depression is a state of sadness or even blankness, with loss of motivation and interest in normal pursuits, changes in appetite and sleep, social withdrawal, and as symptoms worsen, suicidal thoughts. Poor concentration is commonly associated with major depression—but here, the lack of focus is directly tied to the person's mood state. Bipolar disorder, also known as manic-depressive illness, is characterized by severe mood swings, between mania—elation, irritability, and impulsiveness—and depression. Along with ADHD, mania shares impulsivity as a symptom and can also interfere with clarity of thinking and self-control. Yet unlike ADHD, mania is usually recurrent and episodic and is more likely to involve grandiose thinking. It is important to get this differential diagnosis right, as stimulants—a mainstay of medication treatment for ADHD—can make manic states worse.

- **Learning and processing disorders**: These strongly heritable conditions include dyslexia (impaired ability to read), math disorder, and auditory processing disorder (known as APD and sometimes called central auditory processing disorder, which causes difficulty in distinguishing sounds from one another). In these conditions, a student's performance in subjects such as math, reading, and spelling lags behind age expectations (and often, his or her level of general intelligence). People with learning disorders may often be distracted and restless while struggling with challenging learning tasks. ADHD, on the other hand, is more pervasive, revealing itself across a wide range of situations that require effort and focus. Although ADHD interventions, such as medication or behavioral treatments, may help increase the general focus of a child with a learning disorder, they won't be sufficient. More specific strategies are also needed.

- **Trauma**: Beyond official reports to authorities, which tend to be gross underestimates, distressingly high numbers of children are annually victimized by physical abuse, sexual abuse, and/or neglect. These traumas produce a host of physical and psychological effects in youth, including symptoms that can be similar to those of ADHD. What's more, ADHD and trauma may often combine and be related.

Sadly, researchers have found that children with ADHD are more likely to be victims of child abuse by their parents than are typically developing children. Those with ADHD are often quite challenging to raise, and the adults who may have undiagnosed ADHD are likely to be impatient and overly reactive. Although both boys and girls are at risk in this case, research exclusively on girls by Maya Guendelman, during her time as a graduate student in Hinshaw's laboratory, has revealed that girls with ADHD are more likely than other girls to have experienced trauma at an early age. Moreover, these girls are more likely than girls with ADHD who hadn't been mistreated to suffer anxiety and depression and to eventually attempt suicide.

One of the most important tasks for a clinician in such cases is to find out which came first—the ADHD or the abuse—and even more key, whether the abuse is still continuing, as the impact of even the best treatment for ADHD will be of limited help for a child under such circumstances. Often this delicate task will require interviews with a variety of informants so as not to rely on the honesty of a potential abuser. Regrettably, although early editions of the DSM included specific language urging clinicians to obtain information about stressful circumstances and abusive experiences, the current edition omits this important discussion.

Differential diagnosis is also crucial in determining whether any one (or a combination) of several physical ailments listed below may be producing the ADHD-like symptoms:

- **Thyroid imbalances**: The thyroid gland regulates the metabolism of cells. Hypothyroidism, meaning an underactive thyroid, can lead to sluggishness, inattention, and forgetfulness. Hyperthyroidism can make someone restless and distracted.
- **Sleep disorders**: These include insomnia, sleep apnea, and narcolepsy, all of which can result in distracted daytime sleepiness. Making a differential diagnosis is especially difficult in this case, as it's often hard to distinguish the chicken from the egg. Many people with ADHD rarely get a good night's sleep—they may be too busy, worried, or wired—which can compound their symptoms. On the other hand, not getting a good night's sleep is a sure-fire recipe for poor concentration and for anxiety, which can lead to sleeplessness on subsequent nights.

  Scientists have been warning us for years about the importance of a good night's sleep for crucial reasons including our emotional and physical well-being, our ability to learn, and the consolidation of long-term memory. Sleeplessness is especially likely to accentuate a person's focus on the negative rather than the positive. A thorough clinician who evaluates someone for ADHD should make sure to ask about the quality of a patient's sleep and, if necessary, order further tests to investigate it. In some cases, removal of obstructions (e.g., tonsils) can help sleep and ease ADHD symptoms.

- **Allergies:** Allergies can lead to some of the symptoms characteristic of ADHD, including forgetfulness and poor concentration. It's also possible to have ADHD plus allergies, with worsening symptoms in the presence of the allergens.
- **Brain injuries, seizure disorders, and substance abuse**: Certain kinds of head injuries can lead to symptoms that include a lack of focus and impulse control problems. This chain of events can be circular: Early ADHD may lead to impulsive, dangerous actions, resulting in head injuries that compound the initial ADHD symptoms. Mild types of seizures (as opposed to the most familiar and dramatic grand mal seizures that lead to loss of consciousness) must also be considered. These more subtle seizures, known as absence or petit mal seizures, involve short bouts of staring (sometimes combined with blinking or hand gestures), which can be mistaken for the inattentive form of ADHD. In addition, for adolescents and adults, exposure to drugs and alcohol may lead to symptoms resembling ADHD (e.g., loss of motivation related to marijuana use, or cognitive impairment with regular drinking). Of course, as pointed out below, ADHD can also trigger alcohol and substance use, leading to another kind of vicious cycle.

What Additional Disorders or Life Problems Commonly Coexist with ADHD?

Research strongly suggests that well over half of children with ADHD have at least one other psychiatric disorder besides ADHD, and that many of these unlucky souls have two or more such additional disorders. Sometimes these "side orders," also known as *comorbidities*, emerge before or at the same time as ADHD becomes an issue, but at other times they can also be consequences of living with ADHD and the experiences of failure it so often incurs. Thus, it's important to consider the problems described above not only as conditions that mimic ADHD but also as possible accompaniments that require additional treatments.

Overall, about one in three youth with ADHD will experience a significant anxiety disorder and about one in four will have some form of learning disorder. Most children with ADHD do not have major depression or bipolar disorder, but up to one in four or even one in three may develop a mood disorder by adolescence or adulthood.

Tourette syndrome is another close companion of ADHD. Research shows that most children with ADHD do not have this condition, marked by vocal and motor tics, including embarrassing involuntary facial movements, and the propensity to shout out offensive and taboo words. Yet more than half of the much smaller group of individuals with Tourette syndrome have full-blown ADHD.

Still other common accompaniments to ADHD are behavioral problems, chiefly including oppositional defiant disorder (ODD) and conduct disorder (CD). Around 40 percent of all children with ADHD also have ODD, characterized by extraordinarily stubborn behavior, including refusing to obey rules, and defiantly arguing with adults. It's most often kids with the hyperactive-impulsive or combined forms of ADHD who emerge with such patterns of aggression and defiance. (Parents often say they could live with the ADHD if it weren't for the ODD.) Conduct disorder is an elevated form of ODD, encompassing behavior such as fighting, bullying, lying, and stealing. The youth in question may also destroy property, break into homes, and be cruel to animals. As CD escalates, it can lead to serious delinquency. Nearly one in five youth with ADHD—usually adolescents with a long history of early ODD and family dysfunction—will develop CD.

Substance abuse is another unfortunate common partner of ADHD. Considerable research has shown strong links between ADHD and excessive smoking and consumption of alcohol and illegal drugs. Approximately one in four adult patients receiving treatment for alcohol and other drug abuse has ADHD; during adolescence, that number is even higher, nearly one in three. Looking at this differently, approximately one-third of youth with ADHD develop substance abuse by adulthood, well above the national average. Their problems can quickly escalate, as consequences of alcohol, tobacco, and illegal drugs may cause lasting physical and psychological harm.

Children with ADHD are more likely to start smoking tobacco and using and abusing alcohol earlier than their peers and are also more likely to drink excessively. One study found that on average about 40 percent of children with ADHD began using alcohol at around age 15, about double the rate among those without ADHD. The impulsivity and risk-taking associated with ADHD, along with the academic and social failures it can cause, may encourage early and excessive drinking. Similarly, youth diagnosed with ADHD are more likely to experiment with recreational drugs, including marijuana. As marijuana has increasingly been legalized for medical purposes, some doctors have prescribed it for teens suffering the anxiety and anger that can accompany ADHD. To put it exceedingly mildly, we don't believe this is a good idea, as we'll elaborate in Chapter 10.

Sensory processing disorder (formerly called "sensory integration dysfunction") is another diagnosis often linked to ADHD. It's not an official learning disorder recognized in the DSM. Yet some research indicates that as many as 1 in 20 children may be impaired by its symptoms. These can include being oversensitive to sensory input, including not only from the basic senses of smell, sight, sound, touch, and taste but also from others that govern balance and coordination. Some kids can't tolerate bright lights and loud noises such as ambulance sirens, while others refuse to wear certain articles of clothing because they feel scratchy or irritating, even after tags and labels are removed. Still others are distracted by background noises that others don't mind, recoil at an unexpected touch, seem disoriented about where their body is in relation to other objects or people, or have trouble sensing the amount of force they're applying (e.g., ripping a paper when using an eraser). At the other extreme are children who chronically seek *more* sensory stimulation—who may have, for example, a constant need to touch people or textures, fail to understand the boundaries of others' personal space, have an unusually high tolerance for pain, or seem to need to spin or jump around.

It's easy to see how youth displaying these behaviors could be mistaken for those with ADHD. What's more controversial is whether such tendencies are part of ADHD or autism-spectrum disorders, or instead represent something entirely different.

Are there Special Considerations for Diagnosing the Inattentive Form of ADHD?

As we've mentioned, children, adolescents, and adults with the inattentive form of ADHD can more easily slip under the radar, in contrast to the impulsive, hyperactive types who more often get in trouble and annoy people. Even when such individuals come for an evaluation, clinicians may have a harder time pinpointing their problems. Despite their less overt symptoms, however, they've been shown in many studies to have cognitive difficulties, academic failures, and other long-lasting problems on par in severity with their hyperactive peers. They may be suffering in silence, but they're suffering just the same.

Children and adolescents with the inattentive variant of ADHD are often labeled "spacey" or lethargic. They defy the stereotype that youth with ADHD are loud and defiant, and can easily escape the notice of teachers, who are understandably more concerned with more disruptive students. Adults with the inattentive form show particular problems with organization and with executive functions including planning and working memory. A good clinician will take the necessary time to understand such a patient's academic history. If the child or adolescent indeed has the inattentive form of ADHD, it's unlikely that he or she will have been punished for bad behavior but more common that one or more of his or her teachers will have said something like "If only he tried harder . . ." or "She would do so much better if she could only keep track of her materials." The practitioner should also realize differences between inattentive youth and others with ADHD in terms of their social lives. Whereas children with the hyperactive-impulsive or combined forms of ADHD may be rejected by peers, those with the inattentive form may more often be ignored. They don't burn bridges like their aggressive, intrusive peers, but they share the same trouble reading social cues and are likely to be labeled as "weird".

Finally, clinicians need to be on alert for a subgroup of both children and adults who struggle with inattention and distraction and are also unusually lethargic and prone to daydreams. Researchers describe this niche condition as "sluggish cognitive tempo" (SCT), referring to both a mental and physical lethargy. The term is not an official diagnosis as yet and is controversial, especially given its pejorative tone. Yet it has garnered recent clinical interest in that it may signal the need for a distinct diagnosis, apart from ADHD. Research has shown that roughly half of the people scoring high for SCT don't meet the criteria for inattentive ADHD. Much more work needs to be done in this area, especially given that SCT, still so poorly understood, can lead to serious problems in school and at work.

What Can You Do to Make Sure You Get the Best Possible Assessment?

Given the general rule of quick-and-dirty diagnoses—and the unfortunate fact that even some medical professionals still don't believe ADHD is real—it's essential to see someone knowledgeable, well-trained, and experienced, who can examine you or your child objectively and thoroughly, taking the time needed for a valid assessment.

Start by asking your personal physician or your child's pediatrician for a referral to a mental health professional who is qualified to perform an ADHD evaluation. Other parents, teachers, and local ADHD support groups can also be a good source of referrals. And adding new transparency to a historically murky system are websites like Yelp, Healthgrades, and RateMDs.com. Don't trust everything you read on these sites, but it's worth a check before you make that first appointment.

Understand that this is going to be a time-consuming process. Give yourself the advantage of a good education. Finish reading this book, and, if you still have time, some of the other books and websites we list for you at the end. Figure out where you stand on potential treatments, so you won't waste time anguishing in the specialist's office. If the evaluation results in a diagnosis, will you be adamantly opposed to medication or willing to give it a try? Are you prepared to spend the considerable effort required for behavior therapies?

You now know what a good evaluation entails, so prepare to spend time answering many detailed questions about you and your family's history. It will also be worthwhile to figure out your insurance coverage and how much treatment you can afford.

At your first meeting with a specialist, make sure to bring a notebook and pen, or laptop, and have your questions ready.

Focusing On: Diagnosis

It takes careful and thorough assessment to determine whether someone should be diagnosed with ADHD. It's also, necessarily, a low-tech and potentially subjective process that ideally entails a decision by a well-trained professional who has gathered and evaluated input from a variety of sources. One day we may be able to provide patients with a quick blood test or brain scan that would provide a clear answer, but we're not there yet and won't be for the foreseeable future. Computerized attention tests, costly batteries of neuropsychological exams, and IQ and achievement examinations may help to pinpoint underlying cognitive issues but can't provide a definitive diagnosis for ADHD. There is simply no substitute for a thorough analysis of a patient's history and behavior.

A skillful clinician will make sure to investigate whether other mental or physical problems may be causing ADHD symptoms. These can include sleep disorders, thyroid problems, trauma, and anxiety. ADHD medication can help in only some of these cases; in others, it can cause serious problems. A conscientious evaluator will also ask questions about possible conditions that often coexist with ADHD, such as depression, substance abuse, and oppositional or delinquent behavior, as these are all serious problems that may need separate treatment.

5

HOW DOES ADHD CHANGE OVER THE LIFESPAN?

What Does ADHD Look Like in the Earliest Years of Life?

No one ever said it was easy to raise toddlers and preschoolers under the best of circumstances. Most parents quickly understand why the third year of life is known as the Terrible Twos. But imagine living with a child who gave up naps at age 1, goes to bed later and wakes up much earlier than most other kids, and who's constantly on the go—running into the street and playing with anything sharp that may be lying around. Imagine trying to civilize a little boy or girl who stubbornly resists being told what to do, turning the most routine events into escalating power struggles; who terrorizes his or her pre-school teacher, and fellow students, sometimes to the point of being thrown out of the class; and who requires constant supervision to preserve the furniture, not to mention the physical safety of siblings and pets. It's no joke: Children with excess hyperactivity-impulsivity can turn family life into a seemingly endless chain of crises.

Rates of accidental injury for such children are dangerously high, while for their parents so are rates of tension, self-blame, and general misery. Sisters and brothers who don't share the symptoms may be justifiably aggrieved that their overly active sibling requires so much extra attention. In extreme cases, when families are under excessive stress, young children with ADHD are at high risk of being physically abused.

Professional groups including the American Academy of Pediatrics are now calling for recognition and treatment of ADHD as early as age 4. The goal of such early intervention is to help keep families together and calm, reduce injury rates, and ultimately head off what could be years of failure and demoralization.

Although some parents swear they can tell their baby is going to have diagnosable problems from the first sleepless night and although some experts claim they can diagnose ADHD as early as age 2, it's virtually impossible to distinguish extremes of normal development from ADHD behaviors until the child is nearly 4 years old. Not coincidentally, the current professional standards set the age at which a child can be legitimately diagnosed to the time when that child may first need to muster self-control in a preschool class.

As this answer implies, the inattentive form of ADHD typically does not reveal itself until the challenges of grade school are encountered. Problems with speech and language, forgetfulness, the inability to follow directions, lack of focus during play or while listening to a story, and early pre-reading issues may be some of the first indicators of this variant of ADHD in young children.

What are the Typical Consequences of ADHD in Grade School?

Academics

Normally it's by second grade, when teachers first start getting serious about academics and assigning homework, that children with ADHD start to get into real trouble. They can forget to write down their homework assignments, become too distracted to finish them, or, even more frustrating, complete the work but leave it at home on the day that it's due. They find almost anything else to be more interesting and exciting than listening to the teacher or paying attention during reading circle.

Long-term research has shown that more than half of children with ADHD will end up failing at least one grade of school. Although there is at best a very small correlation between ADHD and intelligence—some kids with the disorder may be geniuses, while others are not so bright—students with ADHD on average perform well below normal on standardized tests for math, reading, and spelling. In some cases accompanying learning disorders are to blame, but the classic ADHD problems of inattention, impulse control problems, and lack of self-regulation often suffice.

Social Life

Also by second grade, the social demands at school also start to ramp up. Kids who used to invite everyone in their classroom to their birthday parties become more discriminating. Children start having their own say, overruling their parents about whom they want to come over for a play-date. Cliques start to form, and kids with ADHD—who may be making social blunders by invading others' space and teasing too aggressively—tend to get left out. Parents of children with a history of ADHD report almost three times as many problems with peers as is the norm.

Evidence suggests that kids with ADHD are more often rejected by their peers than children with any other mental or behavioral disorder, including depression, anxiety, autism, or even delinquency. (They develop negative reputations with peers distressingly quickly.) And this is an issue that should never be ignored. In several large-scale investigations of entire school districts, researchers have found that peer rejection during the grade-school years, as reported by classmates, was the single strongest predictor of delinquency, failure to finish high school, and long-lasting mental health problems. In other words, being ostracized by peers was more influential in a child's development than medical conditions, achievement levels, teacher reports of school-related behaviors, and parent ratings of skills and problems. The impact is similar to that of being expelled from school, given that in both situations, the outcast child not only suffers the immediate harm of rejection but is deprived of the conditions to keep learning and improve, academically and socially.

The good news is that researchers have found that even one high-quality friendship can at least partly outweigh the negative impact of multiple rejections from peers. The problem here is that children with ADHD are slower to make friends, more likely to have conflicts with such peers once they do, and have more trouble repairing damaged relationships.

Once you understand just how devastating the social consequences of ADHD can be, you'll likely also realize that finding ways for a child with the disorder to avoid being isolated and rejected must be a key part of his or her treatment.

Family Conflict

The stress load on the parents of children with ADHD—and particularly on mothers, who still provide most of the care—greatly increases when those children are in grade school and first encountering serious problems with teachers and peers. Mothers of children with ADHD, who are so often the target of judgment by teachers and other parents, report that they have far lower levels of self-esteem and markedly more depression, self-blame, and social isolation than mothers of children without ADHD.

Researchers have found that parenting-related stress levels are actually higher for parents of youth with ADHD than for parents of children with autism spectrum disorders. The rates of separation and divorce in such cases are estimated to be at least twice the national rate. Even for parents of children with the inattentive form of ADHD, nightly battles over homework inflict serious levels of wear and tear. One of the most serious problems is that after months or years of fruitless arguing, cajoling, and conflict, many parents of children with ADHD slip into a state known as "learned helplessness," in which they may begin to withdraw from their children, providing little if any supervision during the teen years, when clear limits are more important than ever.

How does ADHD Reveal Itself During Adolescence?

By the teen years, many adolescents who've been diagnosed with ADHD may be noticeably less hyperactive than they were as young children, although roughly three-quarters of those who have been diagnosed will still meet the DSM criteria for the disorder. Many teenagers and adults with ADHD report that although they're less physically active than before, their minds are still revving at high speed. Moreover, recall that ADHD is far more than just hyperactivity: The underlying problems with attention, focus, and general self-regulation often end up causing the most hardships.

As we've noted, problems at school usually become more serious as children transition to middle school and high school, when demands for organizational skills increase. No longer is there just one teacher, and the schedule often changes every day of the week. Responsibility shifts to the student to keep track of homework. The work is increasingly conceptual, and if the basic skills haven't been mastered early on, it's increasingly hard for teens to catch up with their peers.

By age 18, at least three times as many teens with ADHD as those without the disorder will have failed a grade or been suspended or expelled. As we've mentioned, about a third of youth with ADHD quit school before completing 12th grade.

By adolescence, most youth start pushing for more independence, taking more risks, and challenging adult authority. The teen brain is wired to test limits, in an evolutionary press to separate from parents. Yet children with ADHD often carry this natural tendency to extremes. Their sensation-seeking and impulsive personalities come with higher propensities for all kinds of antisocial behavior, including abuse of alcohol, drugs, and cigarettes. All sorts of addictions become dangers in the teen years, including compulsive Internet use and gambling, both for youth with the hyperactive and inattentive forms of ADHD. Teens with ADHD also become sexually active at a younger age than their peers. It's around this time that ADHD first becomes a genuine public health issue, associated with higher than normal rates of teen pregnancies and sexually transmitted diseases as well as car accidents, other fatal and nonfatal injuries, juvenile delinquency, hospital stays, and emergency room visits. Girls with ADHD, as they become young women, are more likely than their peers to suffer physical abuse from their partners.

Mood disorders, self-harm, and even suicide attempts are also risks. All adolescents are more likely to suffer depression than children, but teens with ADHD are at special risk. Youth can become demoralized while brooding over the many failures and social rejections that can come with the disorder. Girls with ADHD are not only at special risk for depression in these years, but also have high rates of eating disorders, especially bulimia, involving bingeing and purging, which is linked with impulse control problems. Male and female teens with ADHD alike are more likely than peers to eat and sleep poorly, compromising their health. Strikingly, teenage girls with ADHD are also significantly more likely than their peers to attempt suicide and to cut themselves as a way to cope with emotional pain. Their impulsivity becomes particularly dangerous in these years, as we explain in more detail in Chapter 6.

Driving, however, is where the rubber literally hits the road. Teen drivers are scary enough—car accidents are the leading cause of death for Americans aged 15 to 19—but adolescent drivers with ADHD can be terrifying. Most of us have trouble resisting the ping of an incoming text on our cellphones while driving, but for adolescents with ADHD, it's simply not a fair fight. Moreover, studies have shown that the mere presence of peers in the car can markedly enhance a teen driver's risk taking; for kids with ADHD, that risk is once again compounded.

During their first few years of driving, teens with ADHD are involved in nearly four times as many car accidents as those without the disorder. They also get three times as many speeding tickets as their peers and are more likely to injure others in accidents. Simulated driving tests have provided substantial evidence of the two devils of inattention (or spacing out) and impulsivity as leading to risky choices, such as trying to run every yellow light. As deaths and injuries from teen drivers have steadily increased, most US states have switched to a graduated licensing system, in which youth learn to drive under progressively more challenging situations. Some states require a three-stage process, starting with a learner's permit, during which a licensed adult must always be in the car with the teen, followed by an intermediate or provisional license and finally by a full license.

Parents should make sure that their teens with ADHD get extra driving practice and delay that trip to the Department of Motor Vehicles as long as possible. It's also wise to keep the risks of driving in mind and make sure that the child is being treated for the disorder, with medication or behavior therapies, well before the 16th birthday.

To what Extent Does ADHD Persist into Adulthood?

A mere generation ago, most experts believed that ADHD symptoms vanished at puberty. Today we know that although it's true that physically hyperactive behavior fades by adolescence, other serious symptoms, including intense mental restlessness, serious inattention, impulsivity, and executive-function-related problems with planning and self-organization persist well into adulthood. Researchers have found that half or more of children with ADHD continue to meet criteria for the diagnosis as adults. And that rate climbs to about two-thirds when diagnosticians collect clinical data from additional informants.

Even when adults no longer meet the full criteria for ADHD, they may still be seriously impaired by accompanying or resulting disorders such as anxiety, depression, substance abuse, antisocial behavior, and gambling or Internet addictions. Their social ties may well be frayed, with high risk for difficulties in intimate relationships, and they may have a bitter history of academic and professional failures. Researchers have found that adults who have been diagnosed with ADHD are up to 14 percent less likely than their peers to have a job. On average, they also earn 33 percent less compared with people in similar lines of work and are 15 percent more likely to be receiving some form of government aid.

The bottom line is that adult ADHD is not only real but has potentially devastating consequences.

How does ADHD Influence People's Self-Esteem?

Like many other things in life, self-esteem—your basic sense of worth—is best experienced in moderation. Utterly low self-worth can be paralyzing, linked to depression and despair. Yet overly high self-esteem can border on narcissism, sabotaging personal relationships.

Intriguing research has revealed that nearly all of us believe we're performing at least somewhat better than average, whether or not that's true. In other words, it's normal and also probably healthy to have a slightly inflated belief in ourselves.

Sadly, however, that's not typically the case for people with ADHD, at least in terms of global self-esteem. Although some are able to maintain a positive view of themselves, research shows that for many others self-esteem starts dwindling after childhood, as failures and rejections accumulate. Such decreasing self-image compounds the symptoms and impairments related to ADHD. At the same time, however, it's also the case that many people with ADHD have the opposite problem of an inflated self-image. Within specific domains, these individuals perceive that they're doing better than what others think or than what objective tests reveal. The clinical term for this phenomenon is "positive illusory bias," and it may predict, understandably, a lack of motivation to change. It's still not known, however, whether it's the inflated self-views or the low performance of these individuals that's the culprit.

But Wait! Isn't ADHD Really a Gift?

Please excuse us if all the worrisome news in this chapter seems depressing. And, yes, there is a contingent of writers and other advocates who maintain that ADHD is a gift. Let's look at some of the reasons they say this.

For one thing, scientists believe that the genes linked to ADHD stem from as far back as hunter-gatherer societies, when it made obvious sense for the survival of the species that a percentage of people would be particularly prone to risk-taking and impulsivity. In such contexts, people with ADHD might be the most vigilant hunters, extra-alert to both potential prey and predators.

The common ADHD trait of novelty-seeking has also been useful in times of dramatic change. For instance, about 15,000 years ago in Asia, when a land bridge was present across the Bering strait, daredevils carrying the DRD4-7R allele were the most likely to migrate to North America. These nomads followed game from Siberia into Alaska, eventually traveling all the way into South America. Researchers have since discovered that the farther one travels down the west coast of North and South America, the higher the concentrations of the DRD4-7R allele (associated with novelty-seeking) that are found in human remains.

Darwin's theory of natural selection suggests that if the DRD4-7R allele and other gene patterns associated with ADHD were inherently harmful for our species, they would have vanished long ago. And indeed, today, several wealthy and famous entrepreneurs, artists and entertainers, and even academics have publicized their childhood problems with distraction and early school failures. Some proponents of the gift theory point out that because ADHD is often a disorder of disinhibition—faulty brakes—it confers an advantage in that one's brain doesn't squelch flights of fancy as quickly as others may do, leading to more potential innovative insights. Albert Einstein has become a poster child for this argument, due to his biographers' portrayal of him as a disorganized daydreamer reportedly late to speak as a tot, who later dropped out of high school. Another frequent example is Wolfgang Amadeus Mozart, described by his biographers as blurting out vulgarities, having verbal and motor tics, and given to composing music while walking, riding a horse, or playing billiards.

Does any of this mean we should go ahead and start calling ADHD a gift? Maybe not, at least not yet. Although CEOs of major firms may claim their ADHD traits make them more creative and less risk-averse, they sometimes omit to add that they are able to thrive thanks to dedicated personal assistants. Nor are they usually eager to dwell on the risk-taking decisions that didn't work out so well. Some of the partners of such CEOs might also tell a different story.

Both JetBlue CEO David Neeleman and Kinko's founder Paul Orfalea (who prefers to call learning disorders "learning opportunities") have credited their ADHD as contributing to their success. Neeleman, who said he thought he was "stupid" all through high school and reported that he spent his adolescence in a fog, watching reruns of *Gilligan's Island*, went on to be the founder of two airlines and be credited for inventing electronic ticketing. On the other hand, he was fired in 2007, after a disastrous week of stranded planes and passengers. Similarly, proponents of the gift paradigm have hailed the Olympic medalist swimmer Michael Phelps for his unusual energy and hyper-focus, although such praise was muted after Phelps was photographed with a bong in 2009 and arrested for drunken driving (twice) several years later.

We'll never know whether Mozart or Einstein might have warranted a diagnosis of ADHD and even benefited from modern forms of treatment. Each life has so many variables. As one biographer has theorized, Mozart's social isolation—a circumstance in his case imposed by his father, who insisted on educating him, but which unfortunately is shared by many people with ADHD—may have slowed his emotional maturity, which never quite caught up with his extraordinary intellect. He was often anxious, lonely, and sad, writing just before his death, "I have come to the end before having enjoyed my talent." Would medicinal or psychotherapeutic support have eased Mozart's pain? Would it also possibly have muted his genius? We'll never know, but what's certain from our perspective is that one of the wisest appraisals of the ADHD gift/curse riddle has come from psychiatrist and author Edward Hallowell, who has described ADHD as a gift that is hard to unwrap. In even the best of cases, it needs a lot of managing and support.

What Contexts Best Suit People with ADHD?

We'll say it again: Context is key for people with ADHD. Although there are no magic settings or professions, we know that it helps a great deal for many students with ADHD to be able to get up and move more than once every hour, and for adults to find jobs with novelty and excitement, combined with at least some structure. Some ADHD experts recommend military service for young adults with the disorder, to help instill discipline; others suggest high-intensity jobs in sales, policing, or entertaining. People with ADHD are overrepresented among self-employed entrepreneurs, often because they may have difficulties with authority or working with others.

Wherever someone with ADHD ends up studying, working, or raising a family, he or she is likely to require a great deal of support and understanding from others, as well as continued engagement in successful treatments. As we hope we've shown, the same traits that can be gifts in certain contexts can also produce risk for conflict and disappointments.

What is the Evidence for Resilience in People with ADHD—that is, the Chance for Positive Outcomes Despite the Symptoms?

It's important to keep in mind that not everyone at risk for the worrisome outcomes we've described in these pages will develop a problem. Certainly, not all individuals diagnosed with ADHD inevitably fail in school, are rejected by their peers, experience high levels of accidental injury, or, by adolescence, have problems with substance abuse, self-harm, or delinquency. A subgroup of people will always manage to beat the odds. Scientists are keenly interested in the traits and circumstances that create such resilience. Although there is at yet a dearth of evidence to answer this question, they've found that such protective factors often boil down to a person's inner traits, including intelligence, a sense of humor, and a perceived stake in the future.

What seem to matter most of all are supportive adults (and peers) in the life of a youth, the building of at least one skill set that can translate into productive work in the future, and adherence to treatments that have proven successful. We'd like to see more studies in this field, together with treatment strategies that aim not just to fix deficits but also to build strengths.

Focusing On: ADHD Over the Lifespan

During the preschool years, ADHD symptoms are difficult to distinguish from the impulsive behavior of many other toddlers. Yet in extreme cases, they can lead to disasters, including family chaos, injuries, and even expulsion from school. A careful clinician can detect when ADHD is the core problem and deploy strategies that reduce the chance of worse outcomes down the line. The majority of childhood diagnoses of ADHD take place in grade school, when differences between children with the disorder and their peers first start to stand out. This is the time when untreated children begin to have problems with homework, lose friends, and possibly start to hate school. Family relationships can also deteriorate, and parents can face overwhelming stress. ADHD can make the teenage years even more taxing, and sometimes catastrophic, as the risks increase of an onslaught including further academic problems, abuse of drugs and alcohol, delinquency, mood disorders, teen pregnancies, sexually transmitted disease, and addictions to gambling and the Internet. A particularly serious danger is distracted and impulsive driving, contributing to traffic accidents that are the number-one killer of adolescents.

By adulthood, as many as half of those diagnosed with ADHD will no longer have conspicuous symptoms, but most will be suffering the fallout in terms of anxiety, depression, divorce, and the toll of academic and professional failures. Self-esteem decreases over time in people with ADHD, who must struggle to avoid either an overly pessimistic sense of self-worth or inflated views about their performance.

Despite all the long-term problems associated with ADHD, enough people with the disorder end up thriving to encourage the view that what's normally viewed as an impairment can be beneficial with the right supports. We're eager for additional research into how these individuals manage to beat the odds, turning hyperactivity into energy, impulsivity into creativity, and daydreaming into innovation.

6

HOW MUCH DOES IT MATTER WHO YOU ARE AND WHERE YOU LIVE?

How Do ADHD Rates Vary Between Males and Females?

An enduring myth about ADHD is that it affects only or mainly boys. For much of the twentieth century, five to as many as 10 boys for every girl were diagnosed with the disorder. More recently, however, girls have been rapidly catching up. The National Survey of Children's Health, a major US survey in 2011–2012—showed that roughly 15 percent of boys have been diagnosed, compared with 6.7 percent of girls, suggesting a ratio of between two and two-and-a-half to one.

We believe that this ratio is a more or less accurate reflection of reality. Although all too many girls with ADHD have historically slipped under the radar, to their detriment, as we explain later on in this chapter, ADHD is in fact more prevalent among boys. For reasons scientists still don't completely understand—but perhaps related to slower brain development in boys—ADHD shares this kind of male predominance with other neurodevelopmental problems that first appear in childhood, including autism-spectrum disorders, serious physical aggression, tics and movement disorders such as Tourette syndrome, and some forms of learning disorders. During the early years of childhood, girls have higher verbal abilities than boys; they are also more compliant, empathic, and socially oriented. It's no surprise, then, that, boys are overrepresented when it comes to childhood mental disorders characterized by social problems (autism), attentional/behavioral symptoms (ADHD), compliance-related behaviors (oppositional defiant disorder, or ODD), and frankly aggressive actions (conduct disorder, or CD).

It's a fact that boys are more at risk during grade school for behavioral problems, particularly of the *externalizing* kind (e.g., noncompliance, aggression, and impulsivity). Yet girls catch up in a different manner during the second decade of life. In the preteen and teenage years, girls are markedly more at risk for so-called *internalizing* behaviors, such as anxiety, depression, eating disorders, and self-injury. It's also at this stage in their lives that many girls end up being seen by a clinician and given a diagnosis of ADHD for the first time.

How Do the Symptoms Vary Between the Two Genders?

The answer to this question is somewhat complicated. Girls who meet the criteria for ADHD are generally likelier than boys to be diagnosed with the inattentive type of the disorder, characterized by day-dreaminess, distraction, and disorganization. Overall, males are typically prone to be more physically active and have more problems with impulse control than are girls.

Many girls with the hyperactive-impulsive and combined forms of ADHD look and act surprisingly like boys with the disorder in terms of impulse-control problems, overactive behavior, and even sheer orneriness, even as their rates of outright violent behavior are much lower. At the same time, girls tend to be hyperverbal rather than hyperactive. Their impulsivity may also take a more subtle form—for example, a young girl who is extraordinarily impulsive may be less likely than a boy to run out into traffic but more likely to indiscriminately pick the first answer on a multiple choice test ("cognitive" versus "behavioral" impulsivity).

As a rule, girls more often than boys are socialized from an early age to cooperate and conform. One consequence of this is that girls with ADHD are more likely than boys to become anxious as they try to compensate for their distraction. Girls typically care more about their school performance—and in general about what others think of them—than boys. Thus, an intelligent girl with ADHD in middle school or high school may succeed in covering up her symptoms with almost obsessive perfectionism but fall apart later when the work becomes too hard to master.

Moreover, just as girls tend to be harder on themselves than boys, evidence suggests that other people, including parents and family members, also judge girls more harshly than boys when inattentiveness and impulsivity promote struggles with typically female areas of competence such as paying attention in class, reading social cues, showing self-control, empathizing, and cooperating. Life can be especially hard for the approximately half of all girls with ADHD who fit the criteria for hyperactive-impulsive or combined forms, because they're more likely to be rejected by peers who judge their behavior as boyish, weird, or out-of-synch with female norms.

What are the Long-Term Consequences of ADHD for Females, Especially When the Disorder isn't Addressed in Childhood?

We've already told you how the rate of girls diagnosed with ADHD has been catching up with that of boys. Now we have another surprise: For women, today's rates are even closer to those of men, roughly on the order of 1 to 1.5 or even lower. What's going on?

We don't know for sure, but can make some informed guesses, based on recent lifespan research. First, however, it's worth a reminder that childhood disorders are mostly based on reports by adults (parents and teachers) whereas adult conditions are diagnosed largely on the basis of self-report. When women reach adulthood, they become much more responsible for their own healthcare and are generally more likely than men to admit to problems. As awareness has grown about female ADHD, more women have been seeking answers to questions that may have mystified them for many years. Many also first begin to suspect they have ADHD after having a child who gets diagnosed.

Another factor tipping the scales is that the inattentive form of ADHD (which, again, is more common in women than in men) appears to be more persistent than the hyperactive-impulsive variant, making it more likely a female adult will still have problems, when for many males, many salient symptoms will have disappeared by then. As we've noted, even when core systems improve, the companion disorders that often accompany ADHD in females—including anxiety, depression, and eating disorders—may persist, eventually encouraging women to get help. Additionally, girls are more responsive than boys, in general, to the pressures and structure of school. Once these supports are gone, young women with ADHD may be more vulnerable to their tendencies to be disorganized.

Overall there's no longer any question today that women experience ADHD at much higher rates than were previously assumed. Beyond the sheer numbers of new diagnoses is the fact that prescriptions for ADHD medications are now rising faster for adult women than for any other segment of the population. Even so, outside of Hinshaw's research, there are few long-term studies of girls with ADHD followed into adulthood, providing little useful research to date on the brain-based differences between female and male symptoms. Still, a sufficient number of girls with ADHD have now been studied to yield a vivid picture of the female version of this disorder. During childhood, girls meeting rigorous criteria for ADHD show serious behavioral, academic, and interpersonal problems, on par with those of boys. As we've mentioned, they are less likely than boys to act out aggressively but more likely to suffer depression, anxiety, and related "internalizing" problems. Some early research revealed that girls with ADHD were more likely than boys to suffer language deficits and other intellectual delays, although more recent studies do not always confirm this contention.

Throughout adolescence, girls are just as likely as boys to experience the major life problems we've described as stemming from ADHD, including academic underachievement and social awkwardness. Their risk for substance abuse may, however, be lower.

Nonetheless, Hinshaw's research, which has followed its participants systematically every 5 years—beginning in the late 1990s, with a 15-year follow-up slated for publication in 2016—has found one especially alarming problem. By early adulthood, a proportion of girls with ADHD engages in self-destructive behavior, including cutting and burning themselves, as well as actual suicide attempts. This high risk has appeared chiefly in those sample members who were diagnosed with the combined form of ADHD when they were girls, suggesting strongly that impulsivity (and the social problems that come with it) plays a strong role here. In fact, almost one in four young women with this combined (inattentive plus hyperactive/impulsive) form of childhood ADHD had made a suicide attempt by early adulthood, and more than *half* were engaging in moderate to severe levels of cutting and other forms of self-destruction. This level of self-harm in girls has not been found with boys or men.

Although girls with the inattentive form of ADHD have comparatively less risk for self-destructive behavior, they do struggle with significant academic problems and a high incidence of traffic accidents due to distraction. In *Understanding Girls with AD/HD*, their classic volume on girls with ADHD, Kathleen Nadeau, Ellen Littman, and Patricia Quinn describe the special hardships for girls with the inattentive type of ADHD as they mature, including perfectionism and social isolation.

What are the Differences in Diagnoses Among Racial and Economic Groups?

The face of American ADHD has been changing dramatically in recent decades. As late as the 1980s, the typical diagnosed child was white, suburban, and relatively well-off. But today, ADHD is no longer an illness of the affluent: African American youth are just as likely as white youth to receive diagnoses and prescriptions. In recent years, ADHD diagnoses of children from families in poverty have outnumbered those of children from wealthier families.

In other words, the former stereotype that cultural deprivation was the only valid explanation for inattentive and disruptive behavior among African American children and adolescents has gone by the wayside. In fact, ADHD appears in all ethnic groups and socioeconomic levels, and rates of diagnosis are now catching up with this reality. A persistent exception until recently, for reasons that aren't entirely clear, has applied to Latino youth. For many years, their rate of diagnosis lagged behind other groups, with national surveys showing that they received diagnoses at about half the rates of other ethnicities. Interestingly, federal researchers have found that children whose families came from Mexico have among the lowest ADHD rates, while those from Puerto Rico more closely match the national average. At the same time, data from the Kaiser Permanente healthcare system in California reveal that Latino rates of ADHD have recently been climbing faster than those in other groups, suggesting that their numbers may eventually catch up.

What Accounts for the Increased Diagnoses Among Racial Minorities and Low-Income Groups in Recent Years?

Many of the same factors that have driven the surge in rates of diagnoses for wealthy and middle-class whites are now boosting rates for low-income minorities. These include the rise in general awareness of the disorder, the reduction (at least to some extent) of stigma, and the loosening of criteria for diagnosis. At the same time, changes in government policy that have also affected white and well-off children have had an outsized impact on diagnoses for low-income minorities.

From 1975, with the passage of the Education for All Handicapped Children Act, the federal government required public schools to accommodate children with disabilities that included documented behavioral, emotional, and learning skills. It wasn't until after much lobbying by advocates, however, that the law was reauthorized in 1991 as the Individuals with Disabilities Education Act (IDEA), which specifically included ADHD in a list of "health-impaired conditions" that could lead to special-education accommodations (see Chapter 2). These valuable school-based supports have included diagnostic testing, special tutoring, resource-room placements, and special day classes (for the most severely affected youth), all free of charge. Not surprisingly, rates of ADHD diagnosis soon rose, as middle- and low-income families who could never have afforded the many thousands of dollars for such services sought special status for their children.

Around this time, the Supreme Court ruled that Supplemental Security Income (SSI) payments to low-income Americans must include those with diagnoses of ADHD and related impairments. Similarly, the US Congress expanded Medicaid coverage to include youth with ADHD. Because this coverage paid for medication (but not behavioral interventions), Medicaid-authorized prescriptions for ADHD rose tenfold within the next decade. In fact, recent national surveys have shown that families receiving Medicaid have been reporting significantly higher rates of ADHD diagnosis in their children than those with private insurance: 14.4 percent versus 9.4 percent. In an even more dramatic turnaround, children in families receiving public assistance for health insurance have recently been 50 percent more likely than privately insured families to have received an ADHD diagnosis.

Added to these factors is the disproportionately high rate of low-birthweight babies—a risk factor for ADHD—in low-income families. This regrettably increasing trend is one reason why we can expect the true prevalence of ADHD (as well as accompanying diagnoses) to continue to rise in at least the near future.

As we've noted, the rates for Latino Americans remain lower, on average, although that trend may not last much longer. The reasons Latinos have delayed in joining the trend are somewhat murky, but probably at least partly due to both a continuing widespread lack of health insurance and a lack of qualified Spanish-speaking physicians. Some researchers have also chalked up the difference to culture, suggesting that extended Latino families may be both more tolerant than other groups of disruptive behavior and less accepting of the stigma associated with diagnosed mental disorders.

How Much Do Rates of Diagnoses Differ Among US States, and Why?

Throughout America, rates of ADHD in children and adolescents vary dramatically among different states. Some Western states have extremely low overall rates of diagnosis—Nevada, for example, has an average of under 5 percent—compared with many Southern states, such as Arkansas and Kentucky, where the rates approach 15 percent. Overall, the South and Midwest, including the Plains states, register much higher rates than the Rocky Mountain and Pacific Coast states. The same patterns hold true for rates of medication as well. In many southern states, a child with ADHD will be twice as likely to receive medication as a child in California.

We told you in Chapter 3 about the strong influence of modern school policies in pushing up the recent rate of ADHD diagnosis. In *The ADHD Explosion*, Hinshaw and his coauthor, Richard Scheffler, made the case that these policies, including the increasing use of high-stakes, standardized tests, have been the single greatest factor in pushing up America's recent rates of ADHD diagnosis, especially among low-income youth. To underline that point, they offered a case study that compared California with North Carolina, where a child is nearly three times as likely to be diagnosed with ADHD.

California, to be sure, has a much larger population of Latinos than does North Carolina, which certainly helps explain some of the difference in the sheer numbers of diagnoses. But the disparity remained even when the authors adjusted for that circumstance. Nor, as they found, did the quality or prevalence of medical care make the difference. It was only when the authors looked at the difference in public-school practices that they found the smoking gun.

Although correlation doesn't guarantee causation, there's striking evidence suggesting that the explanation can be found in the fact that North Carolina, together with 29 other, mostly southern, states, was an early adopter in the 1990s of "consequential accountability" policies that tied school funding to children's scores on standardized tests. Under these policies, school districts had to show increases in students' performance or risk being censured or even closed down. The schools with the most to lose were public schools that served high proportions of impoverished students, eligible for Title I funding and Medicaid. When these policies took effect, ADHD diagnoses surged in these states, outpacing the national trend.

Subsequently, during the 2002–2003 school year, these consequential accountability policies were extended nationally under the federal No Child Left Behind law. As we might expect, the ADHD rates in the remaining 20 states increased rapidly over the next 4 years. In fact, for children from low-income families in public schools that were now for the first time subject to this threat of defunding, rates rose *nearly 60 percent* during that 4-year period. For middle- and upper-class children from those same states, and for those children attending private schools (who were not subject to No

Child Left Behind), the rates of increase of ADHD diagnoses were dramatically lower.

Coincidence? We think not. Rather, we believe that the new accountability laws encouraged school staff to subtly or not so subtly raise the topic of ADHD with the parents of distracted students, hoping that medication might make the difference in performance on the test. For a time in some states, a child with an ADHD diagnosis who was receiving special education could be exempt from the tests (or his or her scores were not counted in the district's average), raising the school's overall scores. But that ended when the practice was outlawed.

After 2009, President Obama's Race to the Top replaced No Child Left Behind, replacing the former sticks with carrots, but still tying federal money to school performance. By 2012, the trend of rapidly increasing ADHD diagnosis for the poorest children in states with accountability laws began to reverse.

How Much Do Rates of ADHD Vary Among Nations Outside the United States?

There's no question that the United States has long been the world capital of ADHD diagnoses, with by far the highest rate of prescription medication. Nonetheless, major international studies suggest the *true prevalence* of ADHD is strikingly similar among developed nations. The United States continues to have the highest rates of diagnostic prevalence, for all the reasons we've explained, while the average rate of ADHD diagnosis among all other developed nations is just over 5 percent of the population of children and adolescents.

As we explained in Chapter 4, one likely reason for the difference is the way we Americans diagnose the disorder, under the relatively loose criteria of the DSM, compared with other nations that use the more restrictive guidelines in the *International Classification of Diseases* (ICD). In addition, some nations require that parents and teachers agree on the presence of a symptom in order for it to count, whereas others require only one source. Others require that the child's problems cause serious impairment before a diagnosis is made. These sorts of diagnostic practices, rather than overall national beliefs, are the key factors making rates of diagnosis higher or lower in a given country.

What's striking is that, outside of subsistence nations (for which ADHD has not yet registered as a concern) and outside of the United States, with its perhaps artificially boosted rates of diagnosis, a remarkably similar proportion of children around the world has clear trouble in handling the demands of classrooms. This fact lends credence to the notion that ADHD is a product of both biological vulnerability and increasing demands for attention and academic performance. When education becomes mandatory, underlying differences in self-regulation and impulse control come to the fore at highly similar levels. ADHD is increasingly a global phenomenon—and one that we predict will remain in ascendancy as international pressures for academic achievement and job performance continue to rise.

What are the Implications as ADHD Diagnosis and Medications Become International Phenomena at Increasing Rates?

ADHD is not solely a biological and cultural reality. In recent years, it has also become an economic concern. As the push for performance, in classrooms and on the job, spreads through the global economy, rising rates of ADHD have inspired concerns about student achievement and workplace productivity and prompted debate about whether increasing rates of medication are justified. Residents of different nations have varied in their response to these questions. Some nations are emulating the United States in providing medication as the front-line treatment for ADHD, whereas others remain resistant. Some nations have instituted school-based accommodations for youth with ADHD, whereas others reject this practice. Particularly intriguing debates are occurring in the population-rich and economically expanding nations of China and India, where academic achievement and vocational productivity are paramount—and where rates of ADHD diagnosis and medication treatment are expanding rapidly.

At this writing, China almost completely lacks school-based accommodations for children with learning and attention problems. Instead, children are expected to accommodate to the lecture-based, many-hours-per-day, extremely high-expectation teaching styles. Diagnosis of ADHD, and treatment with ADHD medications, may be a seriously distracted child's best hope in such circumstances.

Israel presents another example of the consequences of high expectations for academic performance. For a brief period several years ago, Israel allowed stimulant medications to be sold over the counter without any need for diagnosis of ADHD. The practice inspired a public backlash, however, and today only medical specialists are supposed to prescribe medication.

Focusing On: Differences Among Groups

ADHD isn't what it used to be, in America and the rest of the world. For many decades, it was widely assumed in the United States that the disorder was limited mainly to white, suburban boys. Yet in recent years, girls—whose symptoms in general have been harder to detect, although over time they lead to equal or higher rates of impairment—have been catching up rapidly. Today adult men and women have nearly equal rates of diagnoses. A similar story pertains to racial minorities and low-income children: Dramatic changes in awareness and particularly in government policies that provide valuable services have led these groups to start catching up to (or even surpassing) white, affluent youth in terms of diagnoses. One can clearly see the impact of government policies in historic disparities of diagnoses rates among US states. Regions, including the South and Midwest, which were first to institute accountability laws that made school funding dependent on performance on standardized tests, have had significantly higher-than-average rates of ADHD diagnosis—probably related to efforts to treat the disorder and raise test performance. Throughout the world, meanwhile, rising rates of ADHD diagnosis and treatment have accompanied increasing pressure for performance at school and on the job. Speaking of treatment, we'll now move to the second part of this book, a tour of the vast and varied landscape of ADHD interventions, from medication to mindfulness.

PART II

TAKING ACTION

7

HOW HELPFUL—OR
HARMFUL—IS MEDICATION?

How Many US Children and Adults are Taking Medication for ADHD?

In 2015, more than two-thirds of US children and adolescents diagnosed with ADHD were taking medication. By the most recent estimates, that works out to be close to 4 million youth. The vast majority of these children are prescribed stimulants, although other types of medication are also used, as we describe below. In 2010, pharmaceutical firms sold $7.42 billion worth of ADHD medications, up from $4.05 billion just 2 years earlier. Five years later, sales were approaching $10 billion as of this writing—with projections of $17.5 billion by 2020.

As the number of ADHD diagnoses in America has skyrocketed, so has the number of prescriptions. Yet the *rate* of children who take medication has remained fairly steady in recent years, at just above two-thirds of those diagnosed, following a major surge in rates of prescriptions for children through the 1980s and 1990s.

Meanwhile, the number of US *adults* taking prescribed stimulants has quickly risen, to an estimated 3 million by 2015 according to the pharmaceutical company Express Scripts and other projections. The rates of increase are quite high for adult prescriptions, which rose by 53% between 2008 and 2012. An even bigger surprise within this trend is that women of child-bearing age have become the fastest-growing group of consumers of ADHD medications. From 2002 to 2010, the number of annual prescriptions of generic and brand-name forms of Adderall, an amphetamine mix that has become the most popular ADHD remedy, surged among women over 26, from a total of roughly 800,000 to some 5.4 million. Over that same period, the number of prescriptions for women aged 26 to 39 soared by 750 percent, which may suggest an increase in abuse of the medication, as we detail later in this section.

What are the Most Common Stimulant Medications in Use?

Stimulants for ADHD fall into two main categories: *amphetamines*, with brand names that include Dexedrine, Adderall, and Vyvanse, and *methylphenidate*, sold under such brand names as Ritalin, Metadate, Focalin, and Concerta. These two classes of stimulants account for the great majority of ADHD medications today. As we'll describe in more detail throughout this chapter, hundreds of well-controlled investigations—mainly with children and adolescents—attest to the effectiveness of such medicines for ADHD. Studies on adults are fewer in number but also yield clear evidence for stimulant-related benefits.

Another type of medication used mostly for adult ADHD is buproprion, a combination of an antidepressant and stimulant sold under the brand name of Wellbutrin. In recent years, some doctors have also been prescribing modafanil and armodafanil, two closely related vigilance-promoting drugs, or *eugeroics*, sold under the brand names of Provigil and Nuvigil. The US Food and Drug Administration (FDA) has approved modafinil for treatment of people with narcolepsy, shift-work sleep disorder, and excessive daytime sleepiness due to sleep apnea.

Although at this writing neither of these formulas has been approved for ADHD, a number of doctors have been willing to prescribe them "off-label," persuaded by evidence that they can be effective while incurring fewer risks of addiction and abuse than the more mainstream stimulants. Three large studies have shown consistent improvements in children and adults with ADHD who take modafinil. Nonetheless, in 2006, an expert panel advised the FDA not to approve the drug on the grounds that it has a small risk of leading to a potentially fatal skin condition known as Stevens-Johnson syndrome. Although the condition is extremely rare, the panel said it was worth being cautious, given that the risk might increase substantially if even 10 percent of children taking ADHD medications switched to modafinil.

When and How Did Doctors First Begin to Treat ADHD with Medication?

The practice of giving stimulant medications to children diagnosed with ADHD symptoms began with a remarkable accident that took place in the 1930s. At a hospital in Rhode Island, the pediatrician Charles Bradley and his staff had been using a device known as a pneumoencephalogram to study children whose complaints ranged from epilepsy to autistic symptoms to the mysterious condition involving impulsivity and restlessness then referred to as minimal brain dysfunction (MBD).

The arduous, primitive X-ray procedure required subjects to have air injected into their spinal columns and then be rotated about in a specially designed chair. Many of the children in the study suffered nausea and intense headaches, which the clinicians treated with Benzedrine, a prescription amphetamine. To the researchers' surprise, the children not only felt better but also began behaving like little angels, even working more diligently on their math homework. Bradley's reports on this phenomenon led to Benzedrine becoming known as "the arithmetic pill."

The publication of these findings, just prior to World War II, was one of the first twentieth-century instances of a psychotropic medication revealing clear benefits for individuals with certain forms of mental disorder. Treatment with stimulants predated the use of medications for schizophrenia, depression, bipolar disorder, and most anxiety disorders. Nonetheless, it was not until the early 1960s, when the FDA approved methylphenidate (trade name Ritalin), that stimulants began to be widely used for what was by then variably called "hyperkinetic impulse control," "hyperkinetic reaction of childhood," or MBD.

How Do Stimulant Medicines Work to Help People with ADHD?

Stimulant medications can't help everyone with ADHD, but they can improve symptoms in a large majority of children and adults with the disorder. In fact, research has confirmed that stimulant medications can help improve symptoms in 80 or more out of 100 people diagnosed with ADHD, with no discernible difference in response between boys and girls or men or women, or between members of different racial groups. The stimulants boost brainpower, including focus, motivation, and self-control, by increasing the availability of certain of the brain's neurotransmitters—chiefly dopamine and norepinephrine. They can't *cure* ADHD, but they can reduce symptoms while the medication is active in one's bloodstream and brain.

Brain-scan studies have shown that taking stimulants increases the efficiency of the actions of dopamine and norepinephrine in key brain regions and pathways that are essential for self-control, the sensation of reward, and the ability to focus —in other words, the fundamental areas of weakness in people with ADHD. The ADHD expert Thomas E. Brown, at the Yale University School of Medicine, says the medications counter the typical ADHD-related resistance to "motivating oneself to do necessary, but not intrinsically interesting tasks."

For a more detailed picture of how this happens, let's go back to that picture we first described in Chapter 3, of our brains as composed of neurons, or nerve cells. Separating these cells are tiny gaps called synapses. The neurons relay information through the brain via chemical neurotransmitters which travel across the synapses. For this process to work effectively, the neurons must produce and release sufficient amounts of the neurotransmitters, which then must stay in the synapse long enough to react with the receptor molecules of the next neuron in the chain.

After the neurotransmitters are released into the synapse, the excess or unused portion is normally reabsorbed by the neuron that produced it. This work is done by molecules called *transporters*, through a process called *reuptake*. Stimulants, both methylphenidate and amphetamines, block the transporters, slowing down the reabsorption of the neurotransmitters, and thus enhancing their actions on the next neuron in the chain.

The two different types of stimulants work in slightly different ways, and some people respond better to one type than the other. Amphetamines are more potent than the methylphenidate formulas, as they not only block the transporters but also increase the release of neurotransmitters from their storage sites into the synapses. They also make the receptor molecules more sensitive to these chemical messengers.

Because people with ADHD vary greatly in terms of which medication may help them the most, doctors will often need to try out one or two or even more different formulas before finding the best match.

Preschoolers generally respond positively to ADHD medications, although not as strongly as older children and teens. More troublesome, however, is that this age group is more likely to suffer side-effects, which we describe below. For these reasons, US medical professional guidelines recommend trying behavior therapies for preschoolers before resorting to medication.

A resounding confirmation of the upside of stimulant medication came in 1999, with the first published results from the $12 million Multimodal Treatment Study of Children with ADHD. This unprecedented and much-ballyhooed landmark study, known as the MTA, found that medication was more effective than behavior therapy in reducing ADHD symptoms in children—and was nearly as beneficial as a combination of the two. However, as we elaborate later, additional research has suggested that when it comes to helping children fare better in school and socially, medication alone is not nearly as effective as a combination of medication and intensive behavior therapy (see Chapter 8).

A common question when the talk turns to stimulants is, *Why can't I just drink coffee?* Caffeine, after all, is a mild stimulant that can in some circumstances improve focus. The problem is that caffeine (and other *methylxanthines*, the class of drug to which it belongs) is both less potent than amphetamines or methylphenidate and more likely to cause jitters at doses that are truly effective. Its effects don't last long, either. It's better than a placebo, but no panacea.

Another popular misconception is that stimulants work in different ways for people with and without ADHD. Yet in a pioneering study conducted during 1970s, the eminent child psychiatrist Judith Rappaport performed a trial in which preadolescent boys *without* ADHD took Dexedrine (the trade name for dextroamphetamine) for a week. In this placebo-controlled investigation, the boys who took the medication showed significantly better attention and less random physical activity. In other words, the trial showed that a stimulant can provide a small benefit for "neurotypical" children, with larger for effects for children with ADHD.

As we've noted earlier, people with low dopamine activity, including those with ADHD, are underaroused much of the time, and may fidget, seek excitement, or even pick a fight to "wake up" their brains. The stimulants, by promoting the actions of dopamine the actions of dopamine and other chemical messengers in the brain, help to promote arousal and alertness, self-control, and a sense of reward. Probably the most serious common misconception about the stimulants is that they turn children into little robots or "zombies," fostering compliance on rote, boring tasks and making unruly children sit still in dreary classrooms while failing to boost learning. The evidence from considerable research contradicts this assertion. It's certainly true that stimulants make it easier to plow through dull tasks and can improve performance on tests—even raising grades—by increasing the number of academic problems attempted and completed correctly. Yet researchers have also found evidence that they help boost working memory, and even, under the right circumstances, improve complex and creative thinking in children and adults with ADHD. In other words, at their best, they do more than simply keep someone awake to do nonchallenging work.

What are the Chief Pharmaceutical Alternatives to Stimulant Medications?

The FDA has approved two types of medications as alternatives to stimulants for treating ADHD. One is atomoxetine, a selective norepinephrine reuptake inhibitor (SNRI), sold under the brand name Strattera. Similarly to prescribed stimulants, atomoxetine energizes the brain's frontal lobes, which are responsible for self-control but do not mature at the same rates in children and adolescents with ADHD as they do in youth without the disorder (see Chapter 3). Because atomoxetine has little or no effect on dopamine, it doesn't carry the same risk for abuse. At the same time, and although research has shown that its benefits far outweigh those of a placebo, it generally isn't as effective as stimulants, on average. Its major effect is to improve impulse control by blocking the reuptake of norepinephrine.

The second group of nonstimulant ADHD medications consist of blood pressure medications that work in different ways to boost the influence of norepinephrine in the brain and body. These include clonidine, under the brand name Catapres, and guanfacine, marketed as Estulic, Tenex, and in the extended release form as Intuniv. Both have been shown to help improve focus and self-control for people with ADHD who may have trouble tolerating stimulants. These latter medications are also sometimes used in combination with stimulants, to help people with ADHD who have difficulty when the stimulants wear off at the end of the day without impairing their sleep.

What are the Side Effects of ADHD Medications?

Like all medicines, stimulants produce side effects. The boosted influence of dopamine supports alertness and wakefulness, a desired goal when you need to study for hours on end but a problem when you need to sleep. In other words, a common side effect of these medications is loss of sleep, behooving clinicians to carefully monitor the dosage levels and timing of doses. Stimulants also commonly suppress appetite, which is why they used to be prescribed as diet pills. Mild stomachaches and headaches are fairly common, particularly as the body first adjusts to the medication. Stimulants affect the peripheral nervous system, slightly speeding up heart rates and lifting blood pressure by a few points. People with histories of cardiac problems need to be monitored closely when taking these medications. For growing children who take pills over long time periods, ADHD medications may reduce their ultimate height by as much as an inch, probably because excess dopamine activity slows down release of growth hormone. Recent research has produced mixed findings about the duration of this impact, with some studies showing growth suppressed only temporarily and others revealing a more persistent effect, at least in some cases.

The most common side effects of stimulants, including loss of appetite and sleeplessness, often diminish after the first few weeks that someone takes the medication, particularly if doctors work with families and adult patients to calculate optimal formulas, dosages, and timing.

At higher than normal doses, the stimulants can have serious consequences including obsessive behavior, hallucinations, and delusions. We discuss the potential for abuse of these medications later in this chapter.

The most common (yet still relatively rare) reported side effects for modafinil are headaches, nausea, nervousness, rhinitis, diarrhea, back pain, anxiety, insomnia, dizziness, and dyspepsia. Those for atomoxetine include trouble sleeping, dry mouth, decreased appetite, upset stomach, nausea or vomiting, dizziness, problems urinating, and problems with sexual function. Clonidine and guanfacine users have reported dry mouth, dizziness, drowsiness, constipation, and fatigue.

Women who are pregnant should take special care when using any medication and always first check with their doctor. The potential effects of stimulants during pregnancy have not been well studied, but some animal studies suggest that stimulant exposure in utero may lead to behavioral and even neurological problems in the offspring. Erring on the side of caution, doctors agree in most cases that it is best for pregnant women to avoid taking stimulants. Yet in the rare cases where a pregnant woman's ADHD symptoms are truly severe, the clinician must balance the risks to the fetus of exposure to stimulants versus other risks from the mother's impulsive behavior, such as dangerous driving.

Can Taking Powerful Stimulant Medications at a Young Age Harm a Developing Brain?

As ever more and ever younger American children are being diagnosed with ADHD and treated with medication, parents and others have grown concerned over the pills' long-term impact. Some small studies have raised alarms about potential harm from stimulants, with alleged dangers including threats of heart attacks, cancer, depression, and damage to DNA. One by one, however, these studies have been refuted by other, larger investigations. Heart attack risks were found in only a tiny minority of children who had preexisting heart problems, whereas concerns about cancer, depression, and DNA have been debunked by more thorough and careful research. Animal studies suggesting that stimulants could promote later dependence on other medications or drugs turned out to have used different methods from standard clinical treatment of human patients. Specifically, rodents were *injected* with much higher than normal doses, contrasting with the oral doses of stimulants given to children.

The bottom line is that leading ADHD experts today believe that there's no persuasive evidence to date that taking stimulants for ADHD over the long run causes any harm to brains of people with the disorder. In fact, a few prominent researchers have recently gone so far as to suggest that rather than harming the brain in its formative years, stimulants given for ADHD may be "neuroprotective": improving the brain over the long term. Some studies, in fact, have found that on average, youth with ADHD who have taken stimulants for several years have larger brain volumes than those who have never been medicated. (Remember, from Chapter 3, that important brain structures in people with ADHD are on average smaller than those of their counterparts.)

It's important to note, however, that other experts specializing in ADHD, brain scans, and medication contend that claims of long-range positive impacts from the pills on the brain have not been proven. For one thing, the studies cited to support the "neuroprotective" argument haven't relied on gold-standard research methods. Such research would require people with ADHD to be randomly assigned for several years to groups receiving either medication or a placebo, during which time they would have periodic brain scans. These trials would deprive some children of a treatment with established benefits and thus be considered unethical.

What are the "Ritalin Wars"?

As the use of stimulant medications skyrocketed in many regions of the United States, beginning in the late 1960s and 1970s, so did related public controversies. On one side—insisting the meds were both safe and effective—were many leading ADHD experts, many doctors treating the disorder, and teachers and principals who had seen positive impacts on students and in their classrooms. By the 1980s, national advocacy groups such as Children and Adults with Attention Deficit Hyperactivity Disorder (CHADD)—the nation's largest self-help and advocacy group for ADHD—were also championing the medications.

Challenging this perspective and raising concerns about the safety and need for the medications, however, was a diverse group of critics including many thoughtful experts and doctors and conscientious parents. This side of the dispute also included adherents to a school of thought sometimes described as "psychopharmacologic Calvinism," involving the idea that the only mental-health gains worth making are those hard-won through intensive individual or family efforts, in or out of therapy. Proponents of this view argue that medications are a quick fix that may temporarily relieve symptoms without solving the basic problems.

The conflict would probably have never been called a war without the inflammatory and misinformed role of a radical contingent of opponents including the Church of Scientology and its front group, the Citizens Commission on Human Rights, which fervently oppose the entire profession of psychiatry. These groups have campaigned against nearly all psychotropic medications and in 1988 helped fuel a spate of negative press about ADHD medications that led to a temporary nationwide dip in prescriptions and sales. The rebel psychiatrist Peter Breggin, author of *Talking Back to Ritalin: What Doctors Aren't Telling You About Stimulants for Children*, fanned the flames, saying the meds turned children into "zombies." In 2001, Breggin was interviewed on PBS, where he said the meds facilitate "the smooth functioning of overstressed families and schools.. . . It's about having submissive children who will sit in a boring classroom of thirty, often with teachers who don't know how to use visual aids and all the other exciting technologies that kids are used to." Around the same time, the Citizens Commission on Human Rights helped spur plaintiff's lawyers to file half a dozen class-action suits in at least three states against psychiatrists and pharmaceutical firms. Yet all of these suits had been dismissed by 2003.

The ADHD advocacy group CHADD came under fire in the Ritalin Wars on the grounds that it had heavily relied on financial support from pharmaceutical firms. In 2000, plaintiffs in one of the civil cases that was ultimately dismissed named CHADD as a co-conspirator, along with the pharmaceutical firm Novartis and the American Psychiatric Association, in a scheme to "invent and promote" the diagnosis of ADHD so the drug companies could profit from stimulant sales. In recent years, leaders of CHADD have been sensitive to the charges against it. Although the advocacy group continues to support medication as a front-line treatment, it has taken pains to diversify its sources of contributions while also more energetically educating its members about alternatives to medication.

How Long Do Medication Benefits Last?

This is a key question. Recall that in the MTA study described above, scientists discovered that medications outperformed behavior therapy in relieving ADHD symptoms during the active phase of treatment, which lasted one and a quarter years. But during the first year after the treatment phase ended, this advantage tapered to about half its initial effect. After the passage of an additional year, the initial superiority of medication had vanished. In other words, children in all of the randomly assigned treatments were better off than before, but medication did not maintain its initial edge over behavior therapy. Over another dozen years of follow-up, this trend of essentially equivalent improvement has persisted.

The investigators themselves have conceded that they have more questions than answers about these outcomes. Was it that children had stopped taking their medications? (Many indeed had, but this did not tell the whole story.) Had the standards of their treatment deteriorated after they left the rigorous monitoring of the study and returned to their local doctors, who were far less likely to frequently check up on them and adjust dosages? (Probably.) Or were the medications' impacts simply wearing off, at least for some of the kids, as their brains became more tolerant of the boosted influence of dopamine? (This hypothesis still needs more confirmation, but it does appear that for at least some people with ADHD, medications lose their effectiveness over a period of several years. A possible explanation is that over time, as they allow more dopamine to engage with neural receptors, the receptors become less sensitive.)

The follow-up results have received only a fraction of the fanfare surrounding the initial, more optimistic view of the benefits of medication. But their main implication can't be ignored: Although it seems clear that medications can help reduce symptoms in the short run (and maybe over periods of several years), they aren't a panacea and may not be a sustainable solution for all people with ADHD over the course of a lifetime. For the best results, skill-building approaches should be added from the start, although, alas, the US healthcare system rarely subsidizes this optimum combination.

Why Do So Many Teens with ADHD Stop Taking their Medicine?

Researchers have found that American youth on average take their ADHD medications for no longer than 18 months. It's a rule that applies not only to clinically distracted teens but also to people with many other chronic conditions, both psychiatric and medical. Over the long run, inertia often wins, which is surely at least a contributing factor to the long-term weakness of a medication-only treatment plan. Furthermore many people with a variety of chronic physical or mental conditions find it emotionally difficult to keep up with a treatment that's a daily reminder of such illnesses and the stigma that surrounds them.

Even so, it's particularly hard for adolescents to stay on their ADHD meds, such that the rates of medication use drop dramatically during the teen years. Teenagers are famously sensitive to other people's judgment and anxious to fit in with their peers. Many adolescents also say they dislike the sensation of being medicated, which makes them feel constricted, as opposed to spontaneous, creative, and fun. This presents a thorny problem for the teens' doctors and families, given that these years present new dangers, including the risks involved in driving and dating, while schoolwork becomes ever more demanding en route to college applications.

How Should Doctors Monitor Treatment with Medications?

It often takes a good deal of time and experimentation to find the right pill and dose for each person. As noted above, many diagnosed patients have intolerable side effects with the first medication they try, even though there's an excellent chance that a different medication (or different dosage level) may work. Yet some people can't tolerate stimulants at all and need to try a nonstimulant medication. In the first few weeks of testing a new medication, doctors should keep in close touch with their patients and schedule frequent follow-up appointments. Patients and parents of children who receive the medication can help themselves considerably by keeping a medication log to note the size of the dose, time of the dose, benefits, and side effects. Maintaining such records can aid family members and clinicians alike during follow-up appointments.

Once the right formula is found, the dose may need to be adjusted. The initial dose is usually set according to the patient's age and weight, and then raised or lowered depending on feedback from parents and teachers. The best plan is to systematically try a couple of different dosages, obtaining teacher ratings several times per week and using that feedback to help make adjustments.

We emphasize this point because there's little way of knowing in advance which particular medication and dosage will work for any particular individual. Scientists have been trying for years to make such predictions, but to date there's simply no good substitute for trial-and-error testing. In fact, if a particular laboratory comes up with a means of using assessment information (about genes, behavior, cognitive performance, or something else) that could accurately predict who would respond to which medication and which dose, our suggestion is to invest in it—because this would be a major discovery. At present, the best we have is systematic trial and error.

As children grow, they may gradually need higher dosages. And sometimes medications lose their initial effectiveness, requiring adjustments. For drugs of abuse, *tolerance* occurs when—over short periods of, say, just a few days—the dosage must be raised in order to obtain the same "high". Although this phenomenon does not pertain to therapeutic doses of stimulants for people with ADHD, a slower form of tolerance may lead, over many months or years, to gradually increasing dosages (in order to maintain initial gains in behavior or cognitive performance) that ultimately can no longer be sustained. It's one more reason why we strongly recommend behavior therapy for children with ADHD (and cognitive-behavior therapy for adults) as a supplement or substitute for medication (see Chapter 8).

A doctor can help a family decide whether a short-acting medication (lasting a maximum of 4 hours) or a long-acting one (lasting up to approximately 10 hours, depending on the formula and individual) will work best. Some children have problems sleeping when they take the longer-acting medications, but for many others, the advantages of not needing a noontime or after-school dose are enormous. Doctors may also advise families on how and when to take the medication. Given that stimulants can depress a child's appetite, many parents make sure to provide a large breakfast before the pill is taken, and then delay dinner and even offer a bedtime snack to make up for a half-eaten (at best) lunch.

Conscientious doctors will also weigh in on whether the stimulants should be taken all seven days of the week or only on schooldays. On the one hand, medications can help children focus during after-school sports and homework, and for quarrelsome kids, help keep the family peace. But many ADHD experts recommend that children take a break from the medications on weekends, or at least on Sundays, as well as during holidays and summer vacation, in part to make up for any lost growth.

Ideally, doctors should schedule appointments more frequently than once every 6 months or a year. In the MTA study, researchers held weekly visits for the first month, to establish the appropriate dosage, and then scheduled half-hour meetings once per month to meet with the parents and child, while also receiving regular reports from the child's teachers. The MTA doctors also made sure to spend time with the child without the parents in the room for part of the monthly session, to allow the child to speak more freely about his or her attitudes toward the medication. To be sure, this gold-standard schedule unfortunately won't be reimbursed by most insurance plans. Yet without relatively frequent and meaningful visits with your doctor—and by this we mean certainly more frequent than 10 minutes twice a year—the chances of success will be limited.

How Can Patients Improve their Chances of Effective Medication Treatment?

The best first step is to ask for help from your regular doctor, who may recommend a specialist. If you're a parent of a child with ADHD, you're likely to confront an unfortunate dearth of US child and adolescent psychiatrists, meaning that if you want to go that route, you will likely have to wait what could be a long time for an appointment—and/or pay a premium.

Remember that although nonmedical mental health professionals may diagnose ADHD, in all but just a few US states only a medical doctor, such as an internist, pediatrician, or psychiatrist, can prescribe medication. Once you or your child is diagnosed, you may want to continue to see the doctor for prescription checks while also meeting regularly with a psychologist or social worker for behavior therapy—and working with the child's school to implement educational interventions.

You may have to shop around to find someone right for you. Take the time you need. ADHD can take a lifetime to manage. Expect this to be a long-term partnership.

One caveat: Beware of doctors with a lot of pharmaceutical-firm marketing swag in their offices, such as pens, clocks, and calendars bearing the names of stimulants. You're looking for someone informed and skillful but not unquestioningly gung-ho or with a conflict of interest.

How Might Taking ADHD Medication Influence Later Risk for Substance Abuse?

Many researchers have tackled this important question, although at this writing, there's no clear answer amid plenty of conflicting theories. Some experts argue that prescribing medications for behavioral issues teaches youth that pills are a suitable way of coping with life problems. Others worry that the stimulant's action on the reward centers of the brain might precondition patients to become addicted in later life. After weighing the evidence, we believe it's reasonable to suspect that the beneficial effects of medication early on, including the higher likelihood of scholastic and social success, could ultimately help kids avoid risky drug use as teens.

The main reason we still lack good answers to this question is that it's too problematic for a trustworthy randomized test. As we've noted above, such a test would require researchers to deprive a group of children with ADHD, for years on end, of medication that could possibly help them, and thus risk being unethical.

As an alternative, some researchers have tried to find and study groups of children with ADHD who for one reason or another have either stayed on medication for long periods of time or have never used it. The difficulty with this "naturalistic" research is it's nearly impossible to adequately match such groups on variables such as intelligence, academic performance, access to quality medical care, and severity of ADHD symptoms. Thorny questions therefore emerge, such as whether a child who took medications for many years did so because his or her symptoms were initially quite severe. If he or she then ended up with a substance abuse problem, it would be impossible to tell whether this outcome resulted from the medications or the severity of his or her initial problems.

Regardless of such obstacles, several different researchers have attempted such comparisons, producing findings suggesting that taking ADHD medications neither increases nor decreases later risk for substance use and abuse. This overall finding probably results from averaging together results from two (or more) subgroups—one for which a protective benefit truly exists and another in which the medications actually could sensitize the brain to later misuse. Further research will be essential to figure out which particular kinds of youth with ADHD fit into each subgroup.

How Likely is it that People Who Take ADHD Medications Will Become Dependent on Them or Abuse Them?

The danger of dependency is frankly a tricky question. The issue has not been well studied, again because of the problems of performing long-term experimental research on medications versus placebos. The American Society of Health-System Pharmacists has warned that even when taken as prescribed, the medications can be "habit-forming." Yet some research suggests that the danger of psychological dependency may be low. Specifically, when scientists compared groups of children diagnosed with ADHD who took pills with those who took placebos, they found that the youth who took the pills attributed their improved behavior to their personal efforts.

Researchers have also found evidence that stimulant abuse is not a major threat for people with ADHD. For one thing, people with ADHD rarely feel a euphoric high from the stimulants. Instead, and possibly due to their distinct genetic makeup, the medication usually makes them feel subdued, as it works to inhibit impulsivity. This is intriguing, considering that people *without* ADHD are more likely to experience a high on stimulants. Furthermore, it's often necessary to crush and snort or inject the stimulant medications, as with cocaine, to feel such an effect, and in recent years, the ADHD medication market has been dominated by long-acting formulas, which are designed to be crush-proof.

How Much of a Problem is Abuse of ADHD Medications Among People Who Don't Have the Disorder?

This is a cause for concern. In recent years, stimulant medications prescribed for ADHD have acquired a reputation as "smart pills" that can improve productivity and performance for nearly everyone, in school and in the office. Surveys and other estimates show that increasing numbers of people without the disorder, including college students and many students still in high school, take the medication to finish term papers, cram for tests, and stay alert through boring lectures or routine office work.

In a controversial 2009 editorial in the eminent scientific journal *Nature*, seven leading bioethicists and neuroscientists advocated the use of performance-boosting drugs, arguing that "cognitive enhancement has much to offer individuals and society and a proper societal response will involve making enhancements available while managing their risks." Alas, to date, we haven't done a good job at all in managing those considerable risks.

We're all for cognitive enhancement, in principle. One immediate problem, however, is that although it's certainly true that prescription stimulants can help people both with and without ADHD to stay awake and alert longer, the benefits in terms of memory and learning don't seem to be shared. Careful research has shown that for people without ADHD, stimulant effects on learning, in particular, are very small or nil. There is evidence, in fact, that students who abuse prescription stimulants have lower GPAs in high school and college than those who don't. For people with highly developed attention and focus in the first place, stimulant medications may actually hamper learning, and in extreme cases lead to obsessive behavior such as overfocusing and a decrease in flexible thinking. This is on top of the potentially harmful physical effects, such as a risk for heart problems.

At the same time, the much bigger problem for people without ADHD is a considerably greater risk of abuse and addiction. As we've explained above, the medication can provide a euphoric high for people without ADHD, especially when it is crushed and snorted or injected. But even in pill form, there's a much higher chance of addiction and dependence for people without ADHD than for those with the disorder. The best estimates are that between 10 percent and 15 percent of the general population who take ADHD medications illegally will become addicted. This is a far higher rate than for those with the disorder, which appears to be under 1 percent.

The risks of abuse and addiction have multiplied as the rapidly rising numbers of ADHD diagnoses and prescriptions have created an ample supply of stimulants to be traded among friends or sold to strangers. The greatest rates of abuse continue to be found on college campuses, where students use the meds to study—and sometimes party—harder. Dee Owens, director of the Alcohol/Drug Information Center at Indiana University, has told us that Adderall abuse has become "epidemic among young ladies" who are trying to keep their grades up and their weight down and to drink more beer without falling asleep. In widely varying estimates of this illegal trend, researchers have found that as many as 30 percent of college students without ADHD have used stimulants as study aids.

Even more worrisome, however—in what the National Institute on Drug Abuse has called a "cause for alarm"—abuse of prescription stimulants is also becoming more prevalent in high school. An institute survey of 45,000 students found abuse of stimulants had increased among high school seniors, from 6.6 percent to 8.2 percent from 2010 to 2012. In one recent high school newspaper survey of public high school students in affluent Marin County, California, 10 percent of the freshman and *40 percent of the seniors* admitted to having used diverted stimulants.

As increasing numbers of youth, adults, and especially women of child-bearing use the stimulants to boost their productivity, reports of addiction are increasing. Statistics suggest this is an especially tempting trap for young, exhausted, multitasking mothers. Several years ago, the television show *Desperate Housewives* portrayed the risk in an episode in which a mother played by the actress Felicity Huffman tried her kids' Ritalin to help her finish making costumes for the school performance of "Little Red Riding Hood."

Like the Huffman character, many women start out by sampling their children's meds. (It's worth noting here that selling or giving away prescription stimulants is a felony.) Then they get prescriptions of their own, sometimes by faking ADHD symptoms or find the pills by more underhanded means. The human toll of this expanding abuse can be seen in the fact that emergency department visits for stimulant-related complications, including heart problems and psychosis, went up 300 percent between 2005 and 2011 in the United States.

In short, the belief that stimulants can be effective neuroenhancers for people without ADHD is not only misguided but a potential menace to public health, given the dangers of abuse and addiction.

How Do Other Countries Compare with the United States in Medication Prescriptions for ADHD?

As recently as the year 2000, the United States was by far the world champion of ADHD medication prescriptions, home to more than 90 percent of world sales volume. Since then, however, other nations have been quickly starting to catch up, with rates of increase in the use of ADHD meds far in excess of ours. While global sales of ADHD medications rose on average by 20 percent per year from 2005 to 2013, they rose 30 percent annually outside the United States. As an extreme example, in Israel, where awareness of ADHD has been growing dramatically in recent years, the use of two stimulants, Ritalin and Concerta, skyrocketed by 76 percent in 2010 alone.

There are various reasons for this new trend. For one thing, pharmaceutical firms are ramping up their international marketing efforts after having essentially saturated the US market for children and adolescents with ADHD. In Saudi Arabia, for instance, Janssen, which makes Concerta, is the sole sponsor of a website and Facebook page for the Saudi ADHD Society (AFTA), aimed at increasing awareness and treatment of the disorder. A greeting message on the Facebook page says: "ADHD meds help the brain work effectively; they don't make kids zombies. If they do, you should see your Dr. immediately to change meds/dose!"

Moreover, pressures for academic and vocational performance are growing throughout the industrialized world. As we noted earlier, China, in particular, is increasingly pressuring students to improve achievement on tests, even as its schools offer few or no US-style supports for children with learning or attention handicaps. Medication in such cases may be the only resort for students trying to stay alert during routine lectures and classwork.

As a general rule, wealthier nations with higher rates of productivity have higher rates of ADHD prescriptions. Yet a few exceptions exist. Some industrialized nations have policies restricting the kinds of medical professionals who can prescribe such medications. Indeed, even though rates of ADHD diagnosis are remarkably similar internationally (except for the higher rates within the United States), rates of treatment vary—often drastically—as a function of a nation's culture, attitudes, economics, history, and levels of stigma. Brazil, for instance, has traditionally had extremely low rates of diagnosis and medication treatment for ADHD, which some experts attribute to that nation's bitter experience with the use of forced psychiatric medications in earlier, repressive political regimes. France, too, has until recently shown extremely low ADHD diagnoses and rates of medication treatment, largely because psychoanalytic theory remains more popular than treatment by medication.

Focusing On: Medication

The most recent US surveys reveal that nearly 4 million children take medication for ADHD, representing more than two-thirds of all diagnosed children. The net numbers of children and adults taking medication for ADHD have been rising rapidly in recent years, with young women the fastest-growing segment of the market. The most common medications prescribed are stimulants—methylphenidate or amphetamines—although doctors prescribe nonstimulant medications for a minority of people who have the disorder. Stimulants work by helping the brain process two important neurotransmitters: dopamine and norepinephrine. Medication can be a highly effective first-line treatment, but for a variety of reasons, the initial benefits don't last over time in many cases, making other therapeutic strategies all the more important. Evidence suggests that taking stimulant medications does not increase the risk for abuse of other substances in later years, for people with legitimate diagnoses of ADHD. Moreover, the dangers of stimulant addiction for people with ADHD who take the medications are minor, although this is not true for the general population. The use and abuse of ADHD stimulants as "smart drugs" has grown alarmingly in recent years, even as the actual benefits in terms of focus and learning for those without ADHD appear to be quite small. America remains the leader of the world market in stimulants, but as pressures to achieve more in school and on the job spread internationally, other nations are beginning to catch up.

A word of caution here: No matter where you live, make sure you take ADHD medications only under a doctor's supervision. Don't fall into the trap of boosting your dose without consultation. And whether or not you have ADHD, get help right away if you catch yourself lying about your use or getting prescriptions from more than one doctor.

8

HOW HELPFUL IS BEHAVIOR THERAPY, AND WHAT KINDS OF BEHAVIOR THERAPIES HELP THE MOST?

What is Behavior Therapy?

Behavior therapy is the only form of treatment besides medication that researchers have found to be consistently helpful for children and adolescents with ADHD. It can be effective as a substitute for or supplement to medication. Which type of the many different therapies available might be right for your family will depend on factors including the severity and kinds of symptoms involved, your personal tastes and willingness to invest money and time, and, of course, the skills of the therapist.

For the most part, behavior strategies don't involve the stereotypical image of psychotherapy as one-on-one conversations with a psychiatrist, psychologist, or social worker. With the exception of cognitive-behavior therapy for late adolescents and adults, which we describe below, behavior therapy focuses instead on a child's interactions and relationships in his or her daily life, at home and in school. In this case, the therapist's direct clients are parents and teachers, who are coached in the art of using the tools of clear expectations and explicit, frequent rewards, as well as occasional, nonemotional discipline. These incentives work in a somewhat similar way as do the ADHD medications, providing neural reinforcement that helps boost the child's flagging dopamine system.

Finding the right program and therapist is crucial—and tricky. Unfortunately and ironically, our medical system operates under the assumption that in the thick of a life crisis, you'll be able to calmly use your intuition, judgment, and research skills to find the best course of action. Although the system isn't exactly rigged against you, it's not set up to offer maximum support. This is obvious even from the fact that whereas most insurance companies readily cover medication for those diagnosed with ADHD, few will reimburse you for behavior therapy. Another big problem is that as a general rule, skilled behavior therapists for ADHD are few and far between.

Below, we'll describe six different types of behavior therapy, some of which can be combined for the best results. Again, the reward-based behavior therapies work best for children and adolescents, while cognitive-behavior therapy is most appropriate for adults.

What is Direct Contingency Management?

Direct contingency management is a particularly intensive program of behavior modification, in which the daily life of a child with acute symptoms is monitored and managed. It takes place in special classrooms, summer camps, or residential treatment programs, with the settings engineered to immediately reinforce progress, often with points or stickers that can later be traded for coveted goods or privileges.

Several behavioral principles should govern these programs. First, the behaviors that are targets for change should be specific ("make the bed" vs. "clean up"), making it easier to recognize progress. Second, the reinforcement should be immediate—that is, adults must put stickers on the sticker chart as soon as they witness such progress, rather than waiting. Third, adults must make sure that the children are willing to work for the rewards being offered, meaning that kids must be consulted regarding the choice of rewards. Such reinforcers need not cost a lot of money: Some children will work hard just to be able to choose a movie to watch. On the other hand, teenagers usually don't respond well to reward charts—in this case it's better to negotiate in advance how progress will be recognized. Fourth, as emphasized throughout this chapter, it's important to keep expectations low at first, handing out rewards for what might seem like small improvements and then building from there.

Direct contingency management programs outside of the home are usually expensive, due to the small staff-to-youth ratios needed for such regular reinforcement. They have been proven to work well in the short term for youth with ADHD, who lack the intrinsic motivation to finish routine tasks and maintain self-control. Yet the difficulty for children is to maintain their progress once they're out of the tightly managed environment. In fact, this crucial issue about direct contingency management exemplifies a sticking point regarding every therapeutic intervention for ADHD, including both medication and behavior therapy. Both young and older people with ADHD generally have trouble maintaining the gains they can and do make, once the last pill is swallowed or the last reward is delivered. In the case of children, this is what makes it so important for behavior therapists to work closely with families and teachers, training them to keep up a reward-rich environment after the formal therapy ends—and fading out the reward programs only gradually, once intrinsic motivation is apparent.

What Can You Expect from Parent-Training Programs?

Parent training (sometimes called parent management) is the most well-researched behavioral treatment for ADHD. It can help restore peace in conflict-torn families and teach parents how to keep their wits together when dealing with children and adolescents who often seem to be experts in pushing buttons and challenging every limit. Still, like that joke about how many psychiatrists it takes to change a light bulb (just one, but the light bulb really has to want to change), this route requires a willingness to keep an open mind and to work hard to change bad habits that may stem from the parent's own childhood.

To emphasize a key point: Parenting children with ADHD is no walk in the park. Two ADHD experts, Edward Hallowell and Peter Jensen, base their book *Superparenting for ADD* on their belief that parents must provide distracted children with heroic amounts of unconditional love, extra support, and opportunities to excel. On the darker side, psychologist Russell Barkley has eloquently noted that parents of a child with ADHD

> will find themselves having to supervise, monitor, teach, organize, plan, structure, reward, punish, guide, buffer, protect, and nurture their child far more than is demanded of a typical parent. They also will have to meet more often with other adults involved in the child's daily life—school staff, pediatricians, and mental health professionals. Then there is all the intervention with neighbors, Scout leaders, coaches, and others in the community necessitated by the greater behavior problems the child is likely to have when dealing with these outsiders.

In other words, this job isn't for wimps. But parent training can help, and there's no shame in seeking it.

Behavior therapists work directly with the parents, either individually or in a group. They provide education about ADHD, offer exercises in behavior management, model strategies, and teach parents how to maintain records to monitor progress. The record-keeping is important, because one of the key principles of behavior therapy is to strive for gradual change—and it's often hard to know whether things are really changing if the improvement is incremental, and when an occasional explosion can make it seem that all is lost despite overall progress. As noted above, people with ADHD need to choose their rewards and also require a variety of rewards, so it's important to stay ahead of the curve. Also, many busy families have trouble keeping up with such charts, even though they're often essential to make sure that the regular rewards so often needed for kids with ADHD are actually delivered in timely fashion.

One of the main goals for all such parent management programs is to change the tone of the family interactions from hostile and cajoling to positive and encouraging. It's essential to begin with small steps—otherwise, parents and kids alike feel like failures. Any negative consequences to be administered should be done without yelling or sarcasm.

One highly specialized form of parent training is parent-child interaction therapy (PCIT). This empirically based strategy, a mix of behavior therapy, play techniques, and discipline training, features intensive coaching for parents of young children, aged 2–7, with disruptive behavior. Developed in 1974 by the clinical psychologist Sheila Eyberg, PCIT's signature technique is real-time coaching. Parents interact with their children while listening to advice from therapists who watch them from behind a one-way mirror. The goal of PCIT is to get parents to become more skillful in their interactions with children. Specifically, the goal is to be "authoritative": warm and supportive while at the same time able to set clear limits. Advocates of PCIT point to research demonstrating its effectiveness for families of children with behavioral problems. Yet Melanie A. Fernandez, PhD, a New York City clinical psychologist and spokeswoman for the program, cautions that PCIT alone can't substitute for medication. Many children in the program take medication during it and after it ends. Nor does PCIT appear to lessen fundamental ADHD symptoms. Rather, it reduces some of the accompanying issues, such as irritation, anxiety, and depression, that in fact can do the most damage to relationships.

The main goal of all parent training—and of broader family therapy, which we describe in more detail in Chapter 9—is to bring calm and sanity to homes that may have become cauldrons of negativity, coercion, resistance, and punitive discipline, as is all too typical in families with children with ADHD. Parents learn to set clear expectations, to drop their tendencies to yell, to set firm limits and reward or punish behaviors consistently (e.g., through a time-out chair), and to follow through on commands and expectations. Group-based behavior management programs for parents have the advantage that families can learn from others undergoing similar struggles. The therapist can also add individual sessions as needed to tailor approaches to particular family situations.

Ideally, parents learn how to better understand at least some of the reasons for their child's vexing behaviors and to manage their own reactivity. Insights may include realizing that the child with poor working memory simply can't understand a multipart command (like "go to your room, get your gray shirt and comb, and bring them to me"). Parents also learn how to help their children acquire skills, providing rewards for each step of progress. They may also eventually learn how best to manage punitive consequences, such as time-outs and losses of rewards. In general, however, they are coached to use positive encouragement rather than punishment whenever possible.

Parent training can be a special challenge for families of children with ADHD because of the likelihood that a large percentage the parents will have ADHD symptoms themselves, putting them at a major disadvantage in staying organized and controlling their reactions. The best therapists in this field will spend some time helping parents understand their own psychological profile, including ADHD, anxiety, and depression, and also help parents communicate with each other (in two-parent families), given the high odds of marital conflict in families with ADHD. In fact, treatment for the parents' own psychological issues is often a prerequisite for successful parent training.

To increase the potential for success, parent training should be combined with behavior therapy for children in their classrooms, as we describe next. The biggest gains become possible when parents and teachers are aligned about their goals for the child—and provide consistent reinforcement in home and school settings. A danger here is that parents and other caregivers often disagree on the best approach, potentially sabotaging strategies. As a result, it may sometimes be a good idea to include a marital or couples' therapist in the treatment plan.

How is Behavior Therapy Used at School?

The goal here is for the therapist and parent to persuade the child's teacher to join the new behavior-management team, extending the system of rewards to the classroom so that the child gets consistent and mostly positive feedback all day long. It's also crucial for parents and teachers to agree on their goals and expectations.

This type of teamwork may not be an easy sell. Today's teachers are besieged by overcrowded classrooms, low pay, and increasing expectations to produce ever-rising test scores in all of their students. On the other hand, many are also struggling to cope with the disruptions caused by students with ADHD and may be eager to learn better management tools.

An often-effective means of coordinating home and school behavior therapy is a "daily report card" (DRC), on an index card or online. To keep it simple (so as not to ask too much of the typically overburdened teacher), the parents and therapist, working with the teacher, should pick no more than four goals for improvement, such as two academic goals and two behavioral goals, tailored to the child's past performance. For instance, the child's goals for a given week might be to stay in a reading circle for 10 minutes, as opposed to 5 the week before, and to make it through lunch recess without a reprimand from the yard monitor. The teacher simply checks yes or no for each category, depending on whether the child met that day's objectives. Then, when the card goes home, parents tally the responses to add to their reward charts. In an advanced form of this program—with a teacher who's really sold on it—the parents can complete the reverse side of the card with respect to the child's behavior and homework performance during the evening, and the teacher adds the points to the child's reward chart at school.

The goals should be incremental, positive, and as specific as possible. For example, if Jose has been able to work on math problems for only 3 minutes, on average, before wandering away from his desk, the initial objective should be to get him to keep at it for 5 or 6 minutes, rather than the whole math lesson. The technical term for this kind of behavioral shaping is "successive approximations"—and it's one of the most important points to impart to both parents and teachers. After initial successes, the behavioral goals can be made gradually more challenging. But if the child never succeeds in the first place, the program can't be effective.

Beyond the daily reports, there are many ways teachers can give youth with ADHD a better chance of success in the classroom. They can seat the child in the front row in order to limit distractions, give different kinds of prompts and reminders to make sure he or she is following the lesson (sometimes a gentle tap on the shoulder is more than enough), and provide a restless student opportunities to get out of his or her chair, for instance, to pass out papers for the teacher. All of these are possible within regular classroom settings, although in classrooms with more than one or two children with ADHD, a teacher's aide can be a godsend.

For some youth with ADHD, special classrooms or highly structured programs may be needed, a topic we take up in Chapter 9.

Linda Pfiffner's *All About ADHD: The Complete Practical Guide for Classroom Teachers* (see Resources) provides valuable suggestions and strategies for teachers managing classrooms including youth with ADHD.

How Effective are Social Skills Groups for Children and Adolescents with ADHD?

Many schools and after-school programs offer special training for quirky or rebellious kids, with the intention of helping them behave better in class and get along better socially. Many of these classes are taught in a group format, under the reasoning that children and teens are more likely to learn from one another rather than from a lecturing adult.

The problem with this approach, however, is that unless the group leaders are unusually skilled, the classes can degenerate into gripe sessions or, worse, opportunities for the worst-behaving students to tutor the rest in their techniques, bringing the group's behavior down to its lowest level. This kind of "deviancy training," as it's sometimes called, can lead to serious consequences: The negative modeling by peers (especially if it involves aggression or demeaning comments about the adult leaders or peers) may eliminate any hope of progress delivered by the best-intentioned leaders.

Parents concerned about the quality of their children's relationships at school, by which we mean most if not all parents, should treat these groups with caution. Don't hesitate to check the credentials of the group leaders, and make sure they're committed to a structured, reward-based approach, which offers the best chances of success for youth with ADHD. Parents should also be proactive in arranging after-school and weekend play dates for their children with ADHD, who may not initially receive many such invitations. As we've noted, even one supportive friendship can make an enormous difference for such youth.

What Kinds of Programs Can Help Kids with ADHD Get More Organized?

Alas, few public schools offer organizational training for youth with ADHD, even as there is persuasive evidence that they should. A recent large clinical trial based on an organizational skills program developed by the psychologist Howard Abikoff and his team at New York University Medical Center found major benefits for the treated group of third through fifth graders with ADHD.

Abikoff's program is no-nonsense, involving twenty sessions (two per week) delivered individually to the children. Parents sit in for the last 10 minutes of each session, so they can know what skills to reward at home. Units are provided on everything from organizing a desk and backpack to time management (including personal calendars). The treatment also focuses heavily on homework organization, including the recording of homework assignments, packing papers and books needed for homework, estimating time to complete homework, prioritizing homework assignments, and reviewing that their work is done neatly and completely. The researchers compared its benefits with those of a more traditional, parent- and teacher-based behavior therapy model, in which adults were taught to reinforce the children's better organization, time management, and planning, and with a nontreated control group. Both the organizational skills program and the behavior therapy program were far superior to no treatment. Parents rated the children's gains as greater after the organizational skills class than after behavior therapy.

The hope is that such enhanced organization will pay off not only right away but also when the challenges of middle school and high school place a premium on time management and executive functions.

What is Cognitive-Behavior Therapy, and can it be Effective for ADHD?

Cognitive-behavior therapy (CBT) is most often a one-on-one approach in which a therapist helps a patient recognize the connections between his or her emotions, thoughts, and behaviors, and, over time, change the harmful patterns. Unlike traditional psychotherapy, it's focused on the here-and-now, avoiding emphasis on problematic parents, unconscious conflicts, and other ways in which the patient got to be that way in the first place. Researchers have found it to be helpful for late adolescents and adults with ADHD, although not so much for children with this condition, who are usually not sufficiently mature to consciously monitor their emotions and thoughts and translate cognitive change into behavioral improvements.

Cognitive-behavior therapy focuses on getting a person to challenge his or her "scripts," that is, the ways he or she has come to view his or her life and behavior. Normally the therapist won't directly contradict such beliefs by trying to talk the person out of them. Instead, he or she will indirectly help that person see the association between harmful thoughts and behaviors and their usually unpleasant consequences. Ideally, the patient eventually will try out different ways of thinking about and reacting to events, with, again ideally, better results. Patients are taught to monitor their thinking patterns and emotional responses, along with the resultant successes or failures, in order to see for themselves which strategies work best. It's an active approach to treatment: Clients complete homework between sessions to try out these alternative means of construing the world and their own cognitive and emotional responses.

As an example, a client who comes to see the therapist after blowing a job interview may fret that he or she is a loser and will always fail, so what's the use? The therapist would use that opportunity to encourage the client to consider other explanations (perhaps the job simply wasn't a good fit?), to figure out specifically what went wrong (a lack of relevant skills?), and to come up with a plan to make alternative plans for future situations like this. At the same time, the therapist would help the client recognize the association between ruminative (or obsessive) thinking about the failure and how such negative thoughts might lead him or her to give up rather than try again.

Cognitive-behavior therapy for ADHD will also usually involve a structured set of skill-building tasks, aiming, for example, to improve time-management and planning skills, and requiring the client to practice such new techniques outside of the therapist's office.

Research has shown that the goal-oriented nature of CBT makes it one of the most efficient forms of therapy for adults with ADHD. Traditional "talk therapy" has not been proven helpful, as a rule, when it comes to ADHD. In contrast, the active, skill-based approaches of CBT can yield results in a relatively short time, without endless years on the couch. It can also be useful with some of the more common comorbidities of ADHD, such as anxiety and depression.

Which is Best, After All: Medication or Behavior Therapy?

The answer, perhaps not surprisingly, is both. A useful adage is that pills don't teach skills. Although medication for ADHD can reduce symptoms relatively quickly, people who have the disorder—and especially those who are further impaired by accompanying conditions such as anxiety, depression, conduct problems, or learning disorders—often need something more.

The first clear finding on this topic came from the groundbreaking Multimodal Treatment Study of Children with ADHD

(MTA), which we mentioned in Chapter 7. Its initial report in 1999 concluded that carefully monitored and delivered medication was the single best treatment strategy for ADHD, with behavior therapy offering comparatively few additional benefits. It is important to keep in mind, however, that this first report focused mainly on symptom reduction. There was little consideration of family management, social relationships, and success at school, suggesting that the benefits of behavior therapy were probably understated. In fact, a follow-up MTA report, published several years after the initial papers, supports the contention that combining medication and behavior therapy is the best course when considering this broader picture of well-being. Researchers found that only the combination of well-delivered medication plus intensive behavior therapy provided essential benefits for children when it came to relief from comorbid disorders, school achievement, social skills as rated by the teacher, and the family's shift toward a more authoritative parenting style. In other words, most children with ADHD can greatly benefit from behavior therapy, in addition to (or in some cases instead of) medication. In fact, many therapists believe that one of the best uses of the medication is to help patients focus on the behavior therapy, to offer the greatest chance of long-lasting benefits. The hope is for synergy, with the medication enhancing short-term concentration and impulse control and the behavior therapy working to improve long-lasting social and academic skills.

Focusing On: Behavior Therapy

We know we're setting a high bar with our strong recommendation of behavior therapy for ADHD. Obviously such therapy takes a lot more time, energy, and money than does treatment with medications, nor is it easy to find a truly skilled therapist, not to mention someone on your insurance plan. The bottom line, however, is that behavior therapy is usually a must for children and adolescents coping with ADHD. When done right, it can have lasting benefits. Medication can help dampen symptoms, but particularly when ADHD is accompanied by other disorders, such as anxiety, depression, conduct problems, or learning disorders (as is typically the case), the addition of behavior therapy yields a better chance of providing wider and more lasting gains. One of the most effective but also most difficult behavior therapies is parent management training. The goal of this therapy is that families at their wits' end can learn to be both calmer and more skilled at setting limits, two things youth with ADHD urgently need. Ideally, parents and therapists should recruit teachers to help extend the behavior training to the child's classroom. Cognitive-behavior therapy (CBT), which focuses on building skills and changing self-destructive thought patterns, has been shown to be effective in helping late adolescents and adults with ADHD, but doesn't work well with children, who are cannot skillfully monitor themselves without more direct rewards. We continue this general discussion of nonmedication approaches in the following chapter.

9

WHAT OTHER STRATEGIES MAY BE HELPFUL IN TREATING ADHD?

What Do We Know About the Value of Daily Exercise?

The evidence is solid and plentiful on this question: Regular, intense physical exercise is good for everyone's brain and particularly helpful for the brains of people with ADHD. Scientists have known the basic truth about the general benefits of exercise for some years and have found substantial recent evidence to confirm it with regard to ADHD.

In late 2014, the medical journal *Pediatrics* published a study on the cognitive value of exercise, showing that kids who participated in a regular physical activity program showed important improvements in executive functions—including the ability to maintain focus and resist distraction, plus working memory and cognitive flexibility. This study came on the heels of a similar finding in the *Journal of Abnormal Child Psychology*, reporting that a 12-week exercise program improved math and reading test scores in all children, but especially in those with signs of ADHD. Similarly, the *Journal of Attention Disorders* reported that merely 26 minutes of daily physical activity for two months significantly reduced ADHD symptoms in grade-school students.

Outdoor play appears to be particularly helpful. Peer-reviewed research has shown that the children who enjoyed regular outdoor playtime in a green environment had milder ADHD symptoms than other children with ADHD who were stuck indoors. All this dovetails with animal research, which has provided evidence that a lack of play and physical activity can lead to hyperactive symptoms.

The ADHD expert and Harvard psychiatrist John Ratey has written an entire book on the brain-boosting power of exercise, titled *Spark: The Revolutionary New Science of Exercise and the Brain*. He presents considerable research to support his contention that exercise produces, boosts, and regulates substances that relieve pain (endorphins), lift moods and motivation (via dopamine and serotonin), and improve self-control (via norepinephrine). It also helps counteract stress by dampening cortisol, the stress hormone, and improves cellular connections between the cortex and hippocampus that are crucial for learning and memory.

We wonder: Why do scientists have to keep pressing home this point? More importantly, why haven't all American schools understood that it's in their own and their students' interests to provide regular exercise as part of the school day? Although some schools recognize the value of physical education, the trend is unfortunately going in the opposite direction: In many public schools, as students cram for standardized tests, they're barely getting 15 minutes to eat their lunch, never mind take a yoga class or even jog around a field.

We're not saying that aerobic exercise is a cure for ADHD. Still, it should clearly be part of a balanced, overall treatment plan. An added incentive is found in research revealing that increasing numbers of children with ADHD risk becoming obese adults. The lack of attention to diet, as well as impulse control issues, lead to those higher rates of obesity in children with ADHD than in peers without the disorder. Regular exercise—or even any regular physical activity—beginning in childhood could be a preventive strategy.

How Does Diet Affect ADHD?

For decades, many families opposed to medication for ADHD have put their faith in rigorous dietary changes, hoping that these strategies might substitute for pills. The short answer is that considerable research to date shows they can't. No intervention so far matches the strength of ADHD medication or the important benefits of behavior therapies. But that doesn't mean that some nutritional approaches aren't worth trying. Every bit of effort may help, and after many years in which the medical community scoffed at dietary interventions, there's intriguing recent evidence that some may indeed be influential, at least with some people and to some degree.

Beginning in the 1970s, the best-known dietary program for ADHD has been the Feingold diet, developed by the pediatrician Benjamin Feingold, who argued that common food additives including artificial dyes and preservatives worsened or even caused ADHD symptoms. His diet eliminates many food additives and processed foods as well as some fruits and vegetables, including apples, oranges, and pineapple, that contain a kind of chemical called a salicylate.

Feingold claimed that 70 percent of children with hyperactivity benefited from this diet. His claim was made less convincing, however, by the fact that he never compared these children with a control group of youth who were not on the diet, as gold-standard research would require. Moreover, it's important to consider just what it takes for a family to enforce such a diet, monitoring every meal and snack, in and outside the home. In fact, it's hard to tell whether the Feingold diet's touted benefits pertain to the diet itself or rather to the de facto behavior management that families enforcing it must exert, with children gaining indirectly from all that extra attention and structure. Experimental studies in the 1980s, in which researchers rigorously switched regular and additive-free diets in homes, controlling for changes in family structure and expectations, revealed that only a small fraction of children with ADHD (on the order of 5 percent) showed any appreciable response.

In 2007, however, Feingold's focus on food additives received its first major mainstream evidence-based confirmation. Based on carefully designed research funded by the British government, the medical journal *The Lancet* published findings offering "strong support" that additives commonly found in children's diets, including artificial colors and sodium benzoate, appeared to increase hyperactivity. The study persuaded the United Kingdom's Food Standards Agency to call for the removal of six artificial coloring agents from food sold to children. Previously, a meta-analysis of 15 trials by university researchers at Harvard and Columbia had suggested that removing additives from the diets of children with ADHD could be as much as half as effective as treating them with methylphenidate. In 2008, the American Academy of Pediatrics published its own support of the British conclusions, conceding, in its publication *AAP Grand Rounds*, that, "The overall findings of the study are clear and require that even we skeptics, who have long doubted parental claims of the effects of various foods on the behavior of their children, admit we might have been wrong."

Although all of this might motivate any parent to work harder to provide his or her children with an additive-free diet, there are still some big caveats to consider. One is that only a subset of children appear to be sensitive to the suspect chemicals, and it's hard to know which ones they might be. The other major problem, mentioned above, is all the work and discipline required. Backers of the Feingold program and similar approaches usually recommend an "elimination diet," in which a child begins by eating only items in a small group of safe foods, gradually adding more foods to the menu until the symptoms return. This rigorous plan would be difficult for most parents and children to carry out—but may frankly be impossible for many families coping with ADHD. What families can certainly try, however, is to eliminate the most obvious culprits, such as candies, many brightly colored cereals, fruit drinks, and sodas, to see if that helps.

This brings us to another common concern of parents of children with ADHD, which is the worry that sugar in any form may worsen their behavior. The available evidence suggests this simply isn't true. Granted, sugar should be limited in most diets, to protect teeth and maintain a healthy weight. But researchers have found that when it comes to ADHD, sugar has no appreciable effect on symptoms. In one classic study of 35 mothers and their sons, aged 5 to 7, researchers gave all of the boys a dose of aspartame, an artificial sweetener, but told half of the mothers that their sons had eaten sugar. The mothers who thought their children had been given sugar told investigators that they thought their boys became more hyperactive.

Once again, whether or not your goal is to reduce ADHD symptoms, you can't go wrong by giving your child—and yourself—the healthiest possible diet. A couple of eggs or other high-protein dish in the morning beats a chocolate doughnut any day for providing healthy, lasting energy. High-sugar foods indeed cause an insulin response that drives the body's natural sugar levels down within a couple hours, leaving you feeling irritable and stressed.

Which Supplements, if Any, Are Worth a Try?

Our basic rule on supplements is: Proceed with caution. Lots of caution. This thriving, multibillion-dollar industry—a large part of what we call the ADHD Industrial Complex, described in Chapter 10—remains almost entirely unregulated. Supplements are also usually costly and occasionally unsafe. That said, some do merit consideration.

The leader of this pack is omega-3 fatty acids, which you can get by eating more fish, flaxseeds, olive oil, and some nuts, or from capsules of fish oil. A critical mass of credible research indicates that omega-3s can help with attention and moods, although the degree to which they can help is still murky. In a 2009 Swedish study, 25 percent of children with ADHD who took daily supplements of omega-3s had a significant decrease in symptoms after 3 months; by 6 months almost half of the children had improved. Yet a larger, overarching review of relevant investigations in 2011 found only a small yet statistically significant benefit for ADHD symptoms. In other words, there were improvements that were better than could be had with a placebo, but still much smaller than those provided by prescription ADHD medications. This is why we recommend that such supplements should be used, if at all, as an adjunct to but never a replacement for tried-and-true strategies such as medication and behavior therapy.

Still, there is a case for increasing your consumption of these important fatty acids. Most modern diets are deficient in omega-3s, supplying only about 5 percent of what our ancestors consumed. Some evidence suggests that children with ADHD may have even lower levels than the general population, which is unfortunate news, considering the strong consensus that these essential fats not only help prevent heart disease but also support brain health, making neurotransmission more efficient. (They're called "essential" because our bodies don't make them, so we have to consume them.) Some studies suggest that a serious omega-3 deficiency may cause or exacerbate ADHD symptoms by interfering with neurotransmitters, including serotonin and dopamine.

Does that mean that people with ADHD should simply eat a lot more fish? Alas, because our oceans are now so polluted, many species of fish now contain such high mercury levels that they would be toxic if eaten in large quantities. With this caution in mind, a subcommittee of the American Psychiatric Association has suggested that children diagnosed with ADHD eat up to 12 ounces a week of fish and shellfish that are low in mercury, such as shrimp, canned light tuna, and salmon.

If you do choose the supplements, make sure they're puri-fied, and look for a brand with relatively high EPA, or eicosa-pentaenoic acid, compared with DHA, or docosahexaenoic acid. Try to avoid the gummies and chewable form, which tend to have lower doses of these essential ingredients. For younger children, the best strategy may be to buy the liquid form and put it in juice or smoothies.

Fish oil capsules in general are relatively safe and free of side effects, but keep in mind that when taken in high doses, they can thin the blood, preventing clotting. Always consult with your doctor before adding a supplement, especially if you are taking other medications or supplements that might inter-act with them in harmful ways. This includes aspirin, which is also a blood-thinner. The most common side effects of fish oil, which increase with higher doses, are belching, bad breath, heartburn, nausea, loose stools, rashes, and nosebleeds.

Another popular but in this case more controversial sup-plement is gingko biloba, encouraged by prominent experts who recommend it specifically for problems with attention. Animal studies show that gingko biloba can indeed increase the brain's dopamine activity. Yet studies have shown that it also can interfere with blood clotting. Ginseng, another pop-ular purported brain-booster, has been linked to high blood pressure and rapid heartbeat. The bottom line is that to date, no conclusive evidence exists that either of these substances truly reduces ADHD symptoms.

Yet another kind of supplement that has received a lot of attention on ADHD blogs—yet without adequate empirical support—is the amino acid tyrosine, a chemical precursor to dopamine and norepinephrine. Limited research suggests that tyrosine supplements may help control ADHD symptoms, at least in the short term. Somewhat similar is the case of N-acetyl cysteine, or NAC, another touted supplement that comes from the amino acid L-cysteine. Recent research has found it to be potentially useful in treating psychiatric disorders such as addiction and obsessive compulsive disorder, but we have yet to see evidence of its effectiveness in treating ADHD.

Finally, let's look at vitamins and minerals. Here, the evidence is strongest (although not conclusive) for iron, with somewhat less support for zinc and magnesium.

It's indeed worthwhile to make sure that your child, or you, has adequate levels of iron, either from diet, or if needed, a supplement. Intriguingly, a 2004 study showed the average iron level of children with ADHD to be half that of children without the disorder. Because too much iron is dangerous, don't give supplements without first getting a blood test. Dr. Sanford Newmark, author of *ADHD Without Drugs, A Guide to the Natural Care of Children With ADHD*, recommends having a doctor check your child's ferritin levels, which measure the amount of iron stored in the body, cautioning that a normal blood count for iron doesn't mean the ferritin levels are normal. If the levels are low, say below 35, you can talk with the doctor about adding a supplement or, better yet, increasing consumption of iron-rich foods, such as lean red meat, turkey, chicken, shellfish, and beans.

There is also some evidence that zinc and magnesium may help reduce ADHD symptoms. As with iron, both are essential but often lacking in children's diets. Zinc in particular has been found, in limited research, to play a role in improving the brain's response to dopamine and may even help improve the effectiveness of prescription stimulants.

What is Neurofeedback, and How Helpful is it for People with ADHD?

Neurofeedback, sometimes referred to as "EEG feedback," is biofeedback for the brain. The operating theory is that it trains your brain to improve itself through repetitive trials in which you learn to maintain a calm focus. Neurofeedback practitioners claim it can be effective for a vast range of problems, from migraines to anxiety to autism, epilepsy, and ADHD. A major attraction of the technique is the chance that it might help patients from needing medication. Instead, patients practice routines that seem more like exercising a muscle.

The treatment has been growing in popularity even as evidence for such claims has been intriguing but to date not conclusive. What this means, to be blunt, is that trying neurofeedback for yourself or your child amounts to a costly gamble of time and money, with the risk of avoiding other treatments that might be more useful. Practitioners normally require at least 40 sessions, with each session costing more than $100, and most insurance plans won't cover it. Another risk is that the field remains woefully unregulated, meaning you may have to do considerable research to find a conscientious and effective therapist. Alas, many scam artists have jumped into this field.

A typical session looks like this: You sit in a chair while the practitioner attaches electrodes to your scalp with a viscous goop. The electrodes are connected to wires that carry signals from the electrical firing of cells in your brain to a computer. The signals are recorded via an electroencephalogram, or EEG, forming patterns of waves, with different frequencies, the speed of which is measured in cycles per second, or hertz (Hz).

The idea is that your mental states correlate with whatever frequency is dominant, or registering the highest voltage. Slower waves, such as the so-called theta speeds of 4–to 8 Hz, can indicate either drowsiness or an imagination at work. The faster beta waves, from 12 Hz to as high as 35 Hz, correlate with mental states ranging from alert and relaxed to nervous and cranky.

We all need a variety of frequencies to suit different circumstances. But many people have a mismatch of resources to task. The neurofeedback is intended to encourage the right sorts of brain waves while discouraging the less desirable ones. For people with ADHD, a neurofeedback practitioner will usually try to encourage states of calm concentration.

During the neurofeedback session, the patient focuses on a computer screen, which shows images designed to encourage the desired state. One popular program displays images of stars that explode, with enticing music, when you manage to maintain brain waves evidencing a state of calm concentration.

Neurofeedback was developed in the 1960s and '70s, with American researchers leading the way. In 1968, M. Barry Sterman, a neuroscientist at the University of California, Los Angeles, reported that the training helped cats resist epileptic seizures. Sterman and others later claimed to have achieved similar benefits with humans.

The findings prompted a flurry of interest in which clinicians of varying degrees of respectability jumped into the field, some unfortunately making unsupported claims about seeming miracle cures and tainting the treatment's reputation among academic experts. Researchers in Germany and the Netherlands have produced some of the most impressive studies. In 2009, a group of Dutch scientists published an analysis of recent international studies and concluded that neurofeedback for ADHD was "clinically meaningful."

Although such studies strongly suggest that neurofeedback has clinical benefits, at this writing truly definitive studies have not yet been done. In such research, a control group would be hooked up to the same electrodes and see the same images on the computer monitors, but the feedback on the monitor would be false—not linked to the brain waves the clients were displaying at the time. Such a control condition is particularly necessary for a technique like neurofeedback, in which the electrodes and computers often create a strong expectancy that change will occur. In 2014, the National Institute of Mental Health funded a study using just this methodology. Results may not be known until at least 2018. Yet a pilot study also sponsored by the NIMH has suggested that there may be no breakthrough results: Investigators in that case found that both the real and the sham neurofeedback were better than no treatment but no different from each other.

Whether or not neurofeedback provides benefits, questions remain about how long those benefits might persist and whether they would extend beyond a researcher's lab to other contexts, such as a classroom, sports field, or birthday party. Similar questions apply not just to neurofeedback, of course, but to mainstream strategies of medication and behavior therapy. There's simply no silver bullet for ADHD—at least not yet.

Beyond Parent Management Therapy, What Other Help is Available for Families Coping with ADHD?

In contrast to parent training, with its clear goals of helping mothers and fathers calmly shape behavior with structured discipline and rewards and establish clear limits for limit-testing kids, other forms of family therapy deal less with rules and routines and more with improving communication between parents and offspring. A typical premise is that the family is experiencing difficulties not only because of one flawed member but due to the troubled dynamics within the entire family system.

Family conflict is usually a given when one or more members has ADHD. By the time the crew arrives in the therapist's office, mothers, fathers, sisters, and brothers are often coping with considerable anger and blame. The "neurotypical" members may, often justifiably, resent all the attention the member or members diagnosed with ADHD have been getting. They may also be upset at how sloppy and disorganized the child with ADHD may be, which among other things tends to burden others with more chores. At the same time, the person or persons diagnosed with ADHD may feel like the conspicuous target of sometimes unfair blame, a status professional therapists refer to as being the "IP": Identified Patient. A skillful family therapist can help people voice their concerns and resentments and develop a plan to survive the cabin-fever years, before children start to have activities that take them out of the house.

We believe that family therapy can be useful in helping to improve sibling and parent relationships and make home life less nightmarish. Yet given the choice between family therapy and behavior therapy (i.e., the form of family therapy in which parents learn better ways to dole our rewards and set limits), we'd try the behavior therapy first, especially when the child with ADHD is still young. The reason is that whether or not the person with ADHD feels like an IP, they are usually a major source, if not *the* major source, of trouble within the home. As soon as their symptoms improve, you can expect more peace in the family.

Without early interventions, and sometimes even with them, family problems tend to worsen significantly once children with ADHD become adolescents. Any behavior therapy with families in which there's a teen with ADHD must eschew the refrigerator charts that may have worked wonders at ages 7 and 8 and instead focus on skilled negotiations between parents and the adolescent. One strategy worth considering is to draft contracts in which each side acknowledges its particular desires and needs, emphasizing that give-and-take is part of a healthy family life.

One reputedly effective program for families with disruptive teenagers is the Boulder, Colorado-based Vive. It works on two fronts simultaneously, providing parents with a coach while assigning a mentor to the child who is struggling with ADHD or other emotional problems. The mentor, who (like the coach) is a trained therapist, acts as the child's advocate, coach, and sounding board. Vive is aimed at families in serious crisis who can devote substantial time in addition to paying fees of up to $3,000 a month. Most of the appointments take place away from the therapists' office; the parent coach will often visit the family's home to make it easier on working parents, while the youth's mentor may meet him or her at school or at a coffeehouse. A unique aspect of Vive is that the mentor's work extends to helping the youth with school or job-related problems. Similarly, the parent coach will try to help reduce indirect stresses, such as marital bickering and unemployment.

Unlike parent-child interaction therapy, described in Chapter 8, Vive has no independent research to support it. Instead, its leaders point to published research on the potential value of mentors. There is indeed evidence that under the right circumstances—including a highly structured program with expectations of frequent meetings, and good-quality training and supervision of the mentors—this kind of relationship can make a big difference for kids, improving psychological well-being, reducing high-risk behavior, and raising the chances for academic and job success.

Our final example of a family-focused therapy is the Nurtured Heart Approach, a set of strategies developed by the Tucson, Arizona, therapist Howard Glasser, at Tucson's Center for the Difficult Child, beginning in 1994. The gist of the approach is for caregivers to learn to reward a child's good behavior while not unwittingly rewarding bad behavior by overreacting to it. The idea is that difficult kids get stimulated by intense attention and learn to provoke it by misbehaving. Glasser's approach has been used in hundreds of schools throughout the country in the past two decades, including many Head Start programs and several elementary, junior, and high schools in Michigan. The program's website claims it has a "proven, transformative impact on every child, including those with behavioral diagnosis such as ADHD, Autism, Asperger's Syndrome, Oppositional Defiant Disorder, and Reactive Attachment Disorder—almost always without the need for medications or long-term treatment." Nonetheless, at this writing, no controlled evaluations exist of this extremely positive approach to dealing with troubled youth.

What Kind of Academic Support is Available from Schools?

School is often where clinically distracted children suffer the most, but the good news is that there are laws in place that intend to help them. A broad range of school-based accommodations and treatments can benefit kids with ADHD. The big problems are that too many parents still aren't aware of them; school officials can be resistant to spending the money (understandably in some cases, given the stretched nature of public school budgets), and some of the most evidence-based and cost-effective interventions aren't used as they should be.

As a parent of a child with a suspected or confirmed learning disability, including ADHD, you have a legal right to request, and if justified, receive, special support from your child's public school. Section 504 of the US Rehabilitation Act of 1973 is the applicable law in most cases. This piece of civil rights legislation prohibits discrimination based on "mental or physical impairment that substantially limits one or more major life activity," including learning, concentrating, and interacting with others. The law says your child must have "equal access" to education—meaning that if he or she needs more time on tests, note-taking help, tutoring, or even social skills training to stay in school, the school must provide or pay for it.

Public schools must comply with this law on pain of losing their federal aid. On request, the school district is obliged to provide a copy of its Section 504 policies, including an explanation of how decisions may be appealed. The law also allows parents to request an evaluation of their child, which in turn may lead to assistance referred to as a "504 plan." Accommodations under such a plan may include tutoring, counseling, extra time on tests, access to a computer, and an extra set of textbooks to use at home. Active kids may be allowed to sit on "fit balls" or hold squishy toys to control their tendency to fidget. School officials may also encourage a child's teacher to devote extra attention to make sure he or she is engaged in the classroom, to employ more frequent praise and encouragement, and to offer special rewards for progress.

For more severe learning problems, another federal law applies: the IDEA, or the Individuals with Disabilities

Education Act. Under the IDEA, parents have the right to ask that the school screen their child for a disability, potentially a way to avoid paying high fees to a private specialist. If school authorities don't think the tests are needed, they can turn the parents down, but the parents have a right to an appeal. The school's assessments are usually much more limited than those offered by private professionals. Children who qualify under this system are eligible for what's known as an individualized education program, or IEP: a system of accommodations and regular meetings to monitor them. The 504 plan, in contrast, has the advantage of being faster to implement, more flexible, and potentially less stigmatizing.

It's worth remembering that a daily report card can be written in as an accommodation through a 504 plan or an IEP. This is one of the few truly evidence-based accommodations that parents can and should seek.

Unfortunately, many parents these days get into battles with their schools and districts over assessments, diagnostic labels, and the right kinds of accommodations and special education placements for their child. Such conflicts are not only stressful for both sides but drain precious resources from cash-strapped schools that may ultimately be forced by lawsuits to provide costly plans for individual children. We believe that basic behavioral training for more teachers—as well as the use of paraprofessional teachers' aides, who can assist teachers with prompting and rewarding not only youth with ADHD but the whole classroom—could be used much more often than the considerably costlier alternatives of resource rooms, special classes, or even (at the extreme) transfers to special schools, necessarily underwritten by public-school districts. All of these have been outcomes of some of the legal settlements with families of diagnosed children. Advocating for your child at school may inspire you to summon your inner tiger mother, or father, to avoid being intimidated by teachers and other staff. The best course, however, is to be polite and respectful, and not mention the word "lawyer" unless it's absolutely inevitable.

Focusing On: Additional Treatment Strategies

Many high-quality research studies have shown that a regular routine of aerobic physical exercise can make a big difference in the lives of children and adults with ADHD. For as little as a half hour a day, a brisk walk, swim, bike ride, dance class, or many other variations on this theme can improve focus and mood. Exercise can be cheap and effective and good for your body as well as your brain, no matter whether or not you have a diagnosis. We recommend it without reservation as part of your treatment plan, as long as you don't consider it a substitute for evidence-based medication or behavior therapy treatments.

The evidence is weaker when it comes to dietary treatments for ADHD, many of which are nonetheless quite popular. Credible research suggests it's wise to limit or eliminate consumption of food additives and dyes and make sure you or your child is getting sufficient iron, zinc, and omega-3 fatty acids in food or supplements. Beyond that, beware of touted over-the-counter supplements for ADHD, some of which can have dangerous side effects.

Neurofeedback, or biofeedback for the brain, is an increasingly popular intervention for ADHD, with some intriguing research to support it. Nonetheless, it is expensive, time-consuming, and not yet proven to be as effective as medication, behavior therapy, and even physical exercise. It's not yet clear that it will surpass rigorous control conditions; at this writing, the first major US federally funded trial is underway.

Beyond parent training, family therapy may be a useful part of your treatment plan, to cope with resentments that can build up in homes with family members who have ADHD. Accommodations at school should also be part of your overall plan. Federal law makes this a civil right for your child, and some school-based strategies can make a big difference.

10

WHAT DO YOU NEED TO KNOW ABOUT THE "ADHD INDUSTRIAL COMPLEX"?

What Do We Mean by the "ADHD Industrial Complex"?

We use this term to refer to the vast and mostly unregulated marketplace of touted but unproven treatments for ADHD. A few of these may be useful for some people, but most risk costing needless time, energy, and money. Even worse, they may delay or prevent you from exploring evidence-based intervention strategies that would be cheaper and, in all probability, more effective. Considering the long-term impairments linked to ADHD that we've documented earlier in this book, you don't want to waste precious resources and time, missing out on opportunities for yourself or your offspring to make progress toward a better life.

The first rule to follow is: Buyer beware. Later in this chapter we address some of the specifics of being a smart consumer. For now, we'll just say that you'll unfortunately encounter a great deal of hype within the industrial complex. People with ADHD have long been especially easy targets for disreputable salespeople. The same qualities of anxiety, impulsiveness, and carelessness that can make people with this disorder so eager to do *some*thing can also lead to serious mistakes. We sometimes think that Amazon's "one-click" feature was designed with people with ADHD in mind.

What are Some Particularly Egregious Examples of Schemes to Avoid?

Alas, we can think of quite a few of these. Beware in particular of promises that look too good to be true, such as those found in books with titles such as *Dr. Bob's Guide to Stop ADHD in 18 Days*. (As you should know after reading this far, that's simply not possible.) Think again—and then again—before investing in any books or especially in any programs that aren't backed by sound, independent research, which means *most* programs other than traditional behavior therapy for kids, cognitive-behavior therapy for adults, and FDA-approved medications.

A cautionary tale in this regard involves the once-heavily advertised "Dore Program," originally called dyslexia dyspraxia attention treatment (DDAT). The patented technique, touted as effective in ameliorating a range of learning and behavioral problems including ADHD, was developed by the multimillionaire British businessman Wynford Dore, whose daughter had been diagnosed with dyslexia. It consisted of a series of exercises, to be performed for about 10 minutes twice a day, over the course of a year to 18 months. The exercises included throwing and catching a beanbag and standing on a "balance board," a wooden disk that wobbles around on a ball. The purported goal of all this activity was to stimulate the cerebellum, a brain region involved in coordination, timing and possibly some aspects of learning. The first Dore center was established in the United Kingdom in 2000. At its peak, the program was available at dozens of centers in the United Kingdom, Australia, and the United States, with a price tag of $3,500 or more. In 2003, it was favorably featured in a segment on CBS-TV's "60 Minutes II."

Shortly afterward, however, the Dore program came under sharp criticism by scientists and advocacy groups. The International Dyslexia Association declared that such interventions were "not supported by current knowledge," and Dorothy Bishop, a psychology professor at Oxford University, warned pediatricians that published studies on the program were "seriously flawed," and that "the claims made for this expensive treatment are misleading." The Dore organization filed for bankruptcy in 2008, leaving many parents stranded in the middle of their child's program.

One year later, however, the rights to the program were bought by Dynevor Limited, owned by Welsh rugby player Scott Quinnell. A website for the program in 2014 said it was available in Dallas, Texas, and Jackson and Hattiesburg, Mississippi. To say the least, there is no sound evidence behind it.

Diagnostic brain scans are another industrial complex commodity to be avoided, at least for the foreseeable future. In recent years, researchers have learned a great deal about the ADHD brain by comparing hundreds of brain scans of diagnosed children with equivalent numbers of scans of those without the disorder. At this writing, however, the overwhelming scientific consensus is that no one can can tell whether a given person has ADHD simply by looking at an image of his or her brain. That's because there is such great variability among different brains—each made up of over 100 billion neurons and many trillions of synapses—and in different contexts. Indeed, some people with ADHD may not show the expected brain-based differences, even as others who don't have the disorder may do so. The bottom line is that today's technology and level of understanding have not reached the point where it is possible to diagnose *any* mental illness in a given person with a single brain scan.

Regardless, some entrepreneurs, chief among them the author and psychiatrist Daniel Amen, insist that a single scan can be telling. Over the past 25 years, Dr. Amen has built up a large practice based on his contention that he can not only diagnose ADHD but customize treatment strategies based on what he sees on images produced from a single-photon emission computed tomography (SPECT) scan, which uses nuclear imaging to create three-dimensional pictures. He has argued that there are seven subtypes of ADHD (including the "Ring of Fire ADHD" and "Limbic ADHD"), with each requiring a different sort of intervention (chiefly different kinds of medications).

In past years, doctors have used SPECT scans to look at the function of some internal organs, and, more recently, to help evaluate dementia caused by Alzheimer's disease. Yet there is no valid evidence to support the diagnosis and treatment of ADHD in this way. In fact, it would take samples of many *thousands* of brains, in rigorously conducted, long-term clinical trials, to even begin to validate specific treatment profiles for as many as seven subtypes of ADHD, and no one has published this research. Even so, many unsuspecting families have flocked to obtain such brain scans, in order to help their distracted and in some cases aggressive offspring.

Eminent neuroscientists including the University of Pennsylvania's Martha Farah have argued furiously against these sorts of practices. In an opinion piece in the *Journal of Cognitive Neuroscience* titled "A Picture Is Worth a Thousand Dollars"—which actually underestimates the scans' cost—Farah excoriated the practice of relying on such scans not just for diagnostic purposes but for lie-detection and marketing research, writing, "whether from genuine misunderstanding or cynical opportunism, some entrepreneurs are making unrealistic claims about the current capabilities of brain imaging. As cognitive neuroscientists, we have a responsibility to stay informed about this work and to speak up when we see our science being misrepresented."

Perhaps someday far in the future, evidence-based investigators using sophisticated brain-imaging methods may be able, on the basis of voluminous research, to diagnose mental disorders from a scan. For now, we suggest you wait until such a body of evidence exists. The SPECT scans not only aren't cheap—you may find yourself paying up to $3,000 for a pretty image—but require injections of a radioactive isotope, which are potentially dangerous for children.

Can Marijuana Cure Distraction? And—Are We Pulling Your Leg by Even Asking?

As the popularity of medical marijuana has grown in recent years, for recommended uses including chronic pain and nausea from chemotherapy, some doctors have also been prescribing it to treat ADHD, including for adolescent patients. Supporters of this practice, many of whom are concentrated in the San Francisco Bay Area, argue that marijuana is safer and has fewer side effects than commonly used stimulant medications—and that it calms the anxiety and anger that can so often accompany ADHD.

We'd ask them what they were smoking, but we suspect we already know.

Seriously, prescribing marijuana for ADHD is, in general, a terrible idea. Many teens with ADHD understandably wish to be free of the worries and anxieties that plague them and, given their common resistance to stimulant medication treatments (which many, as we've noted, contend make them feel shut down and less creative), gravitate toward such "natural" treatments as smoking weed. Yet any study ever done, with animals or humans, shows that that tetrahydrocannabinol, or THC, the active ingredient in cannabis, disrupts attention, memory, and concentration, the very functions already compromised in people with the disorder.

Researchers have also linked the use of marijuana by adolescents to increased risk of psychosis and even schizophrenia for people genetically predisposed to those illnesses. Regular marijuana use beginning prior to mid-adolescence is reliably associated with loss of IQ points in the following years, even after the use is discontinued. Chronic smoking in adolescence is highly likely to lead to addiction. Even the consent forms handed out by MediCann, a chain of doctors who prescribe medical marijuana in San Francisco, have listed possible downsides including "mental slowness," memory problems, nervousness, confusion, rapid heartbeat, and difficulty in completing complex tasks. "Some patients can become dependent on marijuana," the form specifically warns.

Until the age of 18, patients requesting medical marijuana must be accompanied both to prescribing doctors and to the dispensaries by a parent or authorized caregiver. In some cases, worried parents have helped their children obtain medical marijuana cards so that they wouldn't have to buy the drug on the street or be arrested for illegal possession. Whatever you think of this practice, remember that more than 40 percent of high school students say they've tried marijuana, and there's little a parent can do to prevent that. Frankly, unless the laws change, we understand why parents of impulsive, risk-taking kids would want to minimize the chances of their ending up in juvenile hall on a charge of possession or buy tainted substances on the street.

Nonetheless, we'll repeat: Encouraging chronic marijuana use in adolescents, with or without ADHD, has major downsides. Moreover, there's no good evidence that it helps with the disorder and lots of evidence that it can be harmful. The bottom line: Just say no.

How Helpful are Computer Training Programs?

Computer-assisted brain training has become one of our anxious era's fastest-growing industries. Aging boomers are interested in such training out of the fear that they're losing their edge. Parents of children with learning disabilities have also tuned in, with the hope of finding a way to improve their kids' focus without medication. Researchers have found evidence that some versions of these programs may be effective for preschoolers with ADHD, and neuroscientists and clinicians expect that one day, consistent training in the basics of cognitive performance, including working memory and executive functions, will constitute a solid brick in the foundation of ADHD interventions.

The trick here is to separate the research-backed programs from the considerable hype. Amid a rising number of purportedly efficient brain-training programs, the one that stands out at this writing for having the most substantial research backing is Cogmed, an intensive, 5-week-long plan developed by Swedish researcher Torkel Klingberg in conjunction with Stockholm's Karolinska Institute. The program's goal is to improve working memory (see Chapter 1)—the ability to hold several pieces of information in mind at once, which is often compromised in people with ADHD. Cogmed comes with the twin hurdles of a hefty price and substantial required investment of time. At last check, the program called for its participants to train with the help of a certified coach, usually a psychologist, who can be expected to charge between $1,000 and $2,000. Cogmed also requires a child to complete roughly 40 minutes of training exercises, 5 days a week, for 5 weeks. And this is a lot to ask, given the still-unclear evidence that it can truly help people with ADHD.

Research shows that as a general rule working memory *can* improve with this kind of intervention. Nonetheless, there is still doubt as to whether such gains can translate into real-world academic and social success for people with ADHD. Independent studies of Cogmed have been limited, and recent reviews of research are far more pessimistic than the original claims.

Considerably more speculative are other types of brain-training programs, particularly some of the home-based neurofeedback machines that have been marketed by companies with names like SmartBrain Technologies and the Learning Curve. These entrepreneurs offer equipment purported, respectively, to "pump the neurons" and "make lasting changes in attention, memory, mood, control, pain, sleep and more." A North Carolina firm called Unique Logic and Technology has reportedly sold several thousand "Play Attention" systems, for $1,800 a piece, advertised as "a sophisticated advancement of neurofeedback" to improve a child's focus, behavior, academic performance and social behavior.

The FDA regulates all biofeedback equipment as medical devices. As of this writing, however, the only approved use for any of them is for relaxation. A spokesperson for the International Society for Neurofeedback and Research cautioned that home-based neurofeedback machines should never be used without experienced supervision, given the risk that unskilled use could interfere with medications or prompt an anxiety attack or even a seizure.

What is Coaching, and How Much Can it Help People with ADHD?

A vibrant "life-coaching" industry has emerged in the United States over the past 20 years, with a faction explicitly devoted to people with ADHD. Many adults with ADHD who are adverse to pursuing traditional psychotherapy indeed may be helped by a "coach" who limits the support to practical matters such as time-management, job-performance, bill-paying, and coping with stress while in some cases also working with clients to help set long-term goals. Coaching may be done by phone as well as in face-to-face meetings, offering more flexibility than traditional psychotherapy. Unlike some other forms of therapy, it is not covered by health insurance plans. One influential ADHD coach, Nancy Ratey, says that coaching is based on a "'wellness' model, intended to improve daily functioning and well-being for individuals without significant psychological impairment. This places coaching more in the realm of an educational process as opposed to a treatment process." In other words, people with ADHD who also suffer significant anxiety, depression, or substance abuse, should instead see a licensed therapist.

A major problem with the coaching industry, at least to date, is its overall lack of standards and oversight. There is no specific educational requirement or licensing program for coaches as there is for therapists, including psychologists, psychiatrists, social workers, and marriage and family counselors. Instead, coaches can be certified by any one of several professional organizations, the most formidable being the ADHD Coaches Organization, which has issued guidelines for the types and levels of experience needed to become an associate, full, or master coach. These coaches *can* be certified, that is, but many are not, even as they may still call themselves coaches. More importantly, there has been no rigorously controlled scientific research support for the benefits of coaching, compared to the plentiful support for medication and behavior therapy.

How Useful are Other Alternative Treatments for ADHD?

The list of other unconventional treatments purported to help people with ADHD (as well as with a host of other ailments such as autism and anxiety) is too long to include in its entirety. It features such eclectic strategies as St. John's wort supplements, swimming with dolphins, massage, music classes, acupuncture, and chelation (removal of lead and other minerals from the body). As a group, these fall under the heading of complementary and alternative medicine (CAM), and they are popular with the many Americans who are skeptical or worried about conventional treatment with medication.

The most recent major reviews of CAMs for ADHD conclude, unfortunately, that *none* of the professed interventions—including chiropractic, acupuncture, transcranial magnetic stimulation, anthroposophic therapies, exposure to green space (part of what's called attention restoration therapy), and homeopathy—has enough evidence of efficacy to even come close to being a front-line treatment for ADHD. It's a perplexing world out there in the ADHD industrial complex, and once again, an extremely cautious approach is in order.

What, if Any, Evidence Supports Mindfulness Meditation for ADHD?

"Mindfulness" practices, including meditation and yoga, have been growing in worldwide popularity. A 2007 National Health Interview survey, the most recent such survey available, reported that more than 20 million Americans now meditate regularly and more than 13 million practice yoga. It's reasonable to think that any practice in focusing attention would be helpful for people who have trouble with that skill, and in fact researchers who've studied the question report some intriguing results. In 2008, a team of researchers at the Mindfulness Research Center at the University of California at Los Angeles reported on a pilot study of 24 adults and eight teenagers with ADHD. They found "significant" improvements in self-reported symptoms of ADHD, anxiety, depression, and stress, with the gains continuing 3 months after the training was completed. Although this study lacked a control group, a larger Australian study found similar improvements, while a 2010 pilot study at Duke University found that adolescents and adults with ADHD who practiced mindfulness showed improvement in working memory and the ability to shift attention.

We believe the evidence to date in this field is encouraging but still far from conclusive. Under the right circumstances, there's no question that meditation—and perhaps even better, yoga, for people who have trouble sitting still—can help reduce stress and anxiety, both major problems for most people with ADHD. That's reason enough to add it to your treatment regimen but not to try substituting it for the mainstream strategies of behavior therapy, cognitive-behavior therapy (for adults), and medication.

Some clinicians have been working on extending principles of mindfulness—including thoughtful consideration of alternatives in heated moments and not allowing strong emotions to cloud judgment or compel hasty action—to parent management interventions for families of children with ADHD. Mark Bertin, a pediatrician with strong interest in this area, has produced promising training procedures along these lines, but conclusive evidence awaits sound research.

When Might it Make Sense to Enlist an Occupational Therapist?

An occupational therapist, or "OT," can be a valuable member of a child's treatment team. To be blunt, OTs usually charge much less per hour than a medical specialist or psychologist and can help the child practice and improve a variety of skills including handwriting, tying shoes, catching and throwing a ball, relating to other kids, and organizing a backpack. Typically, an OT will have a master's degree and be professionally certified and licensed by the state government. Some are based at schools, while others work in hospitals and clinics or in private practice.

Sometimes OTs will go beyond the conventional realms of organization and basic coordination to work in other fields, which is where the practice runs into controversy. For instance, some aim to treat issues such as sensory integration problems (see Chapter 4) with practices designed to regulate sensory input, such as controlled spinning movements and balancing exercises. These sorts of endeavors simply don't have evidence to support them. On the other hand, there is good support for other practices that many OTs use to help chronically overwhelmed kids, including tutoring them in taking "sensory breaks" between sessions of stressful deskbound work, or advising them to eat lunch outside if the cafeteria bustle is too much for them.

How Can You Be a Smart Consumer?

There is much you can do to avoid losing out to greedy hucksters and other perils stemming from the ADHD industrial complex.

It starts with your commitment to educate yourself and become an expert on your particular brain, or that of your child. As soon as you suspect that one of you might be affected by ADHD, look for high-quality resources to provide the fundamentals (this book can help, as can the other books and websites we list at the end). And when surfing the web, be skeptical of postings you see on a site that ends with .com. Remember, ".com" means "commercial." Choose .gov or .edu instead.

Next comes the diagnosis. Shop around for your clinician. Seek references from your pediatrician or internist or talk to families who are in the same boat but a few leagues ahead. Or contact your local ADHD support group to ask who's the best mental health professional in your town.

When making the appointment, don't be afraid to ask the clinician or his or her receptionist about his or her experience and leanings (i.e., pro- or antimedication; experienced or not in behavior therapy.) A good question to ask is how many people with ADHD the professional has treated. Queries about educational background and specialty training are important, too. Another valid question, if it seems to be in doubt, is whether the therapist believes the disorder exists!

Organize your questions and concerns before your first meeting. And if after all of your reference-collecting, a doctor or therapist tries to tell you that you either do or don't have ADHD based on a meeting lasting 15 minutes or fewer, don't accept it. Take the time to look for someone with higher standards.

Similarly, when hiring an occupational therapist, don't hesitate to ask for proof of professional accreditation. You can seek a referral through a hospital in your area or check with the American Occupational Therapy Association. Be on the alert for those who translate all symptoms of ADHD (or most other child mental health conditions) to sensory integration issues. Follow a similar path if you try neurofeedback. It's best in this case to start your search for a therapist with a professional network such as the Biofeedback Certification International Alliance.

Don't make any snap judgments about buying or signing up for programs or equipment or books or supplements or classes you see advertised on the Internet. When tempted, give yourself a cooling-off period. And don't ever get on Amazon late at night or after a glass or two of wine.

Focusing On: The ADHD Industrial Complex

The ADHD industrial complex is our term for the ever-expanding marketplace of treatments, programs, services, and commodities on sale purportedly to help "cure" or reduce ADHD symptoms. It's a buyer-beware situation that behooves you to educate yourself and also cultivate sufficient self-control to avoid lurching between promised panaceas. Given the characteristic problems of impulsivity and anxiety, people with ADHD can be particularly easy marks for unscrupulous and unregulated entrepreneurs who've been undeterred by the lack of scientific evidence for supposed miracle-cure herbal remedies, exotic exercise regimens, and purportedly diagnostic brain scans. Some of the methods we describe above, including occupational therapy sessions and coaching, may work wonders for some people. Nonetheless, we include them in this chapter dealing with more speculative approaches because of both the lack of empirical evidence to support them and because individual therapists in this field can vary so greatly in the way they do their jobs. Similarly, we address cognitive training in working memory in this section—even though it has some supportive evidence—because we believe that its benefits have been exaggerated by purveyors. The risk in all of these more questionable strategies is that you can easily waste a lot of time, energy, and money by pursuing these schemes that would be more wisely invested in evidence-based treatments such as behavior therapy, cognitive-behavior therapy, and medication.

11

CONCLUSIONS AND RECOMMENDATIONS

Can America's Rate of ADHD Diagnoses Continue to Grow?

Indeed, it can. Even as, currently, a shocking one in five American boys has been diagnosed with ADHD, we believe this rate could escalate to one in four, or—in a worst-case scenario—even one in three over the next decade. In fact, in a few southern states, the rate for boys is already that high. Hold onto your seats and consider some of the powerful factors spurring this growth:

- **Performance pressures in US classrooms show little sign of abating.**
  Admissions to top colleges are ever more difficult to obtain, especially considering the continual increase in national and international competition. As teenagers and their families seek an edge, increasing numbers of them may seek a diagnosis to get accommodations on college-entrance exams and placement tests—as well as access to medication designed to boost performance.
- **Adults have become the fastest-growing market for ADHD diagnoses and medications, and they have lots of room to catch up with kids.**
  Adults have yet to be diagnosed at rates approaching the likely prevalence of ADHD for their age range.

- **Preschoolers have become a brand-new market.**
  In 2011, the American Academy of Pediatrics released guidelines that lowered the age at which children can be diagnosed with and treated for ADHD. Guidelines for the previous decade had covered children only beginning at age 6, but the new rules lowered that to 4. The Academy said it was acting on emerging new evidence that makes it possible to spot the disorder at an earlier age and emphasized the need to start treatment as soon as possible. Another factor sure to increase preschool diagnoses is huge interest and substantial investment in pre-K and transitional-K programs nationwide. As preschool enrollment expands, ever-increasing numbers of distracted preschoolers will be required to sit still under the scrutiny of their teachers. Without careful attention to this new constituency, ADHD diagnoses could soar in the post-toddler set.

- **It's easier than ever to get a diagnosis.**
  In the latest step in what has been a continuing trend, the most recent edition of the *Diagnostic and Statistical Manual*, the DSM-5, released in 2013, further relaxed the required criteria to be diagnosed with ADHD. For example, symptoms can now have first occurred before age 12 instead of by early childhood. Also, instead of requiring impairment in more than one setting, clinicians now must find only that several symptoms are present in more than one setting. For anyone aged 17 or older, only five symptoms are now needed instead of the six previously required and still needed for younger children. Some of these changes are based on research findings, even as they lower the bar for diagnoses.

- **Growing numbers of premature and very small babies are being born—and surviving.**
  Recall that low birthweight is a contributing cause of ADHD. From 1980 to 2006, the percentage of infants born with low birthweights increased slowly and steadily, to reach 8.3 percent of all births, although that trend

has since appeared to level off. Research suggests the increase in multiple births after 1980, in part due to more women seeking fertility treatments, contributed to this trend, while the rate of low birth-weights among singleton newborns also grew. As medical procedures improve, more babies are surviving risky pregnancies, with many being born prematurely and at low weights.

- **Expanding access to healthcare insurance makes it likelier than ever that more clinicians will be identifying and treating ADHD.**

  If the Affordable Care Act continues to survive legal and judicial challenges, it could become one of the greatest spurs to increasing ADHD diagnoses. In its most relevant mechanisms, which tip the scales toward more use of services, the new national law extends coverage to young adults under their parents' policies, levies penalties for failures to obtain health insurance, expands Medicaid, and requires coverage for preexisting conditions.

In light of all these factors, it's more than likely that ADHD diagnoses and treatment, including new prescriptions for medication, will continue to increase in the United States—a bellwether for the rest of the world. The biggest potentially countervailing factor would be a popular backlash against the seeming epidemic and in particular against the cursory diagnoses that have undoubtedly inflated the overall rates of diagnosis. That backlash could come from any one of several directions. In particular, if abuse of stimulant medication continues to increase and claims more casualties, public alarm might force professional groups to tighten restrictions for diagnosis and treatment. At the same time, national academic testing firms and college proctors may react to perceived exploitation of the diagnosis and tighten their own eligibility requirements for accommodations.

Another potential countervailing force could come in what economists call "demand shock," as increasing numbers of

Americans seek assessments and treatments from a dwindling supply of trained professionals. Even more, if the economy slips into recession once again, and in particular if out-of-pocket costs for medical care increase, ADHD diagnosis and treatment may come to be viewed as a luxury.

Considering the sum of all these of these forces, our prediction is that this locomotive won't slow down any time soon. Still, we expect—and would welcome—a leveling off and even decline over the next several years to levels that are found in the rest of the world. Although we surely encourage people with genuine problems to seek a diagnosis and treatment, we'd also dearly like to see more rigorous assessments and tighter requirements for accommodations to shut off the spigot of questionable diagnoses.

How are Big Pharmaceutical Firms Influencing the Surge in ADHD Diagnoses?

Hmm, let's count the ways. Big Pharma has been aggressive and ingenious both in and outside the United States in marketing its wares to treat ADHD. Major pharmaceutical firms have sponsored research, paid generous consultant fees to leading experts in the field, pressed medication samples on pediatricians, contributed hefty sums to national advocacy groups such as Children and Adults with Attention Deficit/Hyperactivity Disorder (CHADD) (the annual conferences of which are rife with brand-name banners, tote bags, and other pharma-paraphernalia), and even sponsored a Facebook page for mothers of children with ADHD. The everyday consumer, however, is most likely to encounter this influence in glossy advertisements in popular magazines, such as *People*, showing Norman Rockwellian scenes of seemingly happily medicated children doing chores or homework.

We hope we don't sound too cynical. But the fact is that only two developed nations at last count—the United States and New Zealand—allow pharmaceutical companies to directly advertise prescription medications to consumers. Prior to the late 1990s, the only advertisements for medications were found in medical journals. In a major shift, the Food and Drug Administration made it much easier to target ads directly to consumers, in a policy it argued would increase competition and consumer choice. Since that time, direct-to-consumer (DTC) ads have become a multi-billion-dollar annual enterprise, as US pharma firms have taken maximum advantage of their opportunity.

We grant that the ads, extending to the Internet and TV, have helped make treatment available and have major potential to reduce shame and stigma. But we also worry that these ads have been a big factor in pushing up the rates of overdiagnosis of conditions including ADHD. The advertisements for ADHD medications tend to flourish at the time of release of expensive, new, patented medications, and then subside when less-expensive generic formulations of the medication come to the market.

Medical journals in particular have profited from this revenue stream. As the *New York Times* noted in a 2013 article titled "The Selling of Attention Deficit Disorder," a prominent publication in the field, the *Journal of the American Academy of Child and Adolescent Psychiatry*, went from no ads for ADHD medications from 1990 to 1993 to about 100 pages per year a decade later. The *Times* described a 2009 ad for the nonstimulant drug Intuniv as showing a boy in a monster suit taking off his hairy mask to smile at the camera. "There's a great kid in there," the text read. The medication's many side effects were listed, as required, but in exceptionally tiny print.

Other pitches to consumers have been subtler. McNeil Pediatrics' ADHD Moms Facebook page featured seemingly mainstream mothers boasting about the benefits of medication for their children. You had to look closely to see that the page was being sponsored by a medication firm. "After dinner one night my son sat and played with Lego for hours it seemed, he looked so happy, peaceful, and I turned to my husband

and said, 'We did good,'" wrote Michelle Goodman-Beatty, a mother of four, and one of the page's more than 8,000 "fans." Elsewhere, the page had a mother claiming that ADHD medications reduce the chance of substance abuse—a claim that as we've noted has not been borne out by research. The page also featured comments from a pediatrician counseling mothers to keep their kids taking their stimulants on weekends, holidays, and school breaks, which is far from the consensus of many ADHD experts, who suggest that children take medication breaks.

Beginning in the year 2000, the Food and Drug Administration has repeatedly chastened pharmaceutical firms for false and misleading ads and on several occasions required such ads to be withdrawn—instructing drug companies to cancel them for being false and misleading or exaggerating the effects of the medication. As the *New York Times* has reported, Shire agreed in early 2013 to pay $57.5 million in fines partly stemming from charges of improper advertising (including unwarranted claims about benefits) of several medications, including Vyvanse, Adderall XR, and Daytrana, a patch that delivers stimulant medication through the skin.

What Impact, if Any, Have State Policies Had in the Rise in Diagnoses?

In Chapter 6, we described one big way that state policies have made a difference in recent years: Those states that prioritize test scores via accountability legislation had a quick jump in diagnoses, particularly for low-income youth, as schools put pressure on their most distracted students to be diagnosed and treated.

More recently, however, some US states have joined a backlash against the growing numbers of diagnoses and prescriptions by instituting laws to try to stem the tide. Some of these laws have been inspired by parents' lobbying of state officials in the wake of notorious cases involving the medications. In one widely publicized case in 2000, for instance, a county medical examiner in Michigan blamed Ritalin for the heart attack that killed a 14-year-old Michigan boy named Matthew Smith, who had been taking the medication for the previous 10 years. That same year in Connecticut, the New Canaan school district told Sheila Matthews that her son, then 7 years old, had ADHD and needed to be given medication. Matthews resisted the guidance and instead cofounded an alliance against schools' involvement in diagnoses.

The backlash in state agencies and legislatures began in 1999, when the Colorado State Board of Education passed a resolution urging school personnel to use academic solutions rather than psychotropic drugs to resolve problems with behavior, attention, and learning. This was followed by at least 45 other bills and resolutions, with laws that have passed or are still pending in 28 states.

Beginning in 2001, a particularly resolute group of 14 states, with Connecticut leading the way, enacted laws specifically attempting to strengthen the rights of parents who refuse to medicate their children and to curb the influence of teachers and schools in promoting such treatment. The states have tackled these issues chiefly with three strategies: statutes that specifically prohibit school employees from recommending medication, bans on school requirements that children take psychotropic medications as a condition of enrollment, and guarantees that a family can't be charged with child neglect for refusing to medicate a child.

These laws have had major impacts. The 14 states that enacted them have been marked exceptions to the rapid increase in ADHD diagnoses throughout the rest of the United States. In fact, rates of diagnosis remained flat in these states from 2003 to 2012, even as they rose sharply in the rest of the nation.

Our own view on this subject is that teachers must be part of the assessment of any child for ADHD. Without such information, it's all but impossible to determine whether a student is sufficiently impaired in the classroom to validate a diagnosis. At the same time, the vast majority of teachers is not adequately trained to be trusted to counsel parents on medication treatment and shouldn't be doing so.

What Needs to Be Done to Foster Greater Understanding of the Reality of ADHD in Girls and Women?

In Chapter 6 we detailed some of the potentially serious consequences for girls and women with ADHD whose symptoms are sufficiently subtle to escape diagnosis and treatment. Given both the comparative difficulty in detecting ADHD in young girls (versus boys), and the particular dangers of girls' developing comorbid problems, such as anxiety, depression, eating disorders, and self-harm, we believe there should be much more research and media focus on feminine ADHD in the years to come. Specifically, mental health professionals, school employees, and parents must become more aware that girls can and do suffer the symptoms of ADHD, even as many such girls' symptoms include comparatively subtle difficulties with organization and focus rather than severe impulsivity or hyperactivity.

One challenge here is that while poster boys and poster men for ADHD have become fairly familiar (think David Neeleman, Jim Carrey, Michael Phelps, and James Carville), the same can't be said for successful women with ADHD, although Paris Hilton's name keeps coming up. This makes it hard to emphasize the serious risks of the disorder while showing that happiness and achievements are still possible. Efforts to build awareness in this realm should also emphasize that the same major evidence-based treatments work just as well for girls and women as they do for boys and men.

Out of concern for the special hardships faced by females with ADHD, some mental health experts have advocated special treatment for women and girls that would include redefining the disorder. Their suggestions have included expanding the list of symptoms to include "hyperverbal" behavior that is more commonly observed in girls and to require fewer symptoms to diagnose ADHD in girls. To justify such a change, however, we believe researchers need to show that lower symptom thresholds in females are linked to high levels of impairment. So far, the research on this issue is mixed.

Any change in the way we define ADHD brings up a dilemma. On the one hand, girls shouldn't be held to the same diagnostic standards as boys if doing so means that many truly impaired children can't get help. On the other hand, any further loosening of standards for a diagnosis may risk opening the floodgates even more at a time when many children are already being diagnosed unnecessarily. We're therefore not great fans of changing the standards for ADHD, even as we do think a lot more could be done to raise awareness of the special hardships faced by girls with the disorder, in order to make sure they are identified and helped.

What Do Today's High Rates of ADHD Say about Our Culture? Is this a Warning Sign We Need to Address?

If you've been reading between the lines up until now, you should easily guess the answer to this one. Yes, we believe it's a warning sign. The startling rates of increase in this disorder—and in particular, in the obvious *over*diagnosis of ADHD throughout America—speaks volumes about the state of the United States in the twenty-first century.

To be sure, some of the signs are truly positive. The high rates of ADHD tell us that millions of families are now braving the stigma of mental illness to seek help for their children—and that perhaps, in the process, shame and silence are starting to abate. They tell us that doctors have learned a lot more about how to identify and help people who were previously completely at the mercy of a truly impairing disorder. They also tell us that many of us are embracing the difficult challenge of trying to understand the variability of human brains—and that, in many cases, we're willing to adapt our expectations and, at least in some cases, our classrooms and job sites, to accommodate such differences.

At the same time, as we head into a future in which it's not impossible that more than one in four boys will end up with an ADHD diagnosis, we have to understand that apart from all the incentives to get diagnosed these days (including government aid and accommodations at school), there may just be a major mismatch between our evolving brains and the way we live our lives. An obvious problem, too, is the increasing air and water pollution that, as we detailed in Chapter 3, may be contributing to the numbers of births of children with ADHD. These high rates are also telling us that we need to do more to provide better prenatal care so as to reduce the high rates of babies with low birth-weights and potentially rein in extravagant fertility treatments that can lead to multiple births. The rising rates of ADHD are additionally telling us that we need to do more to reduce the high numbers of teenage pregnancies and to improve nutrition for pregnant mothers. Better education for expectant parents about smoking and alcohol use during pregnancy is a related and essential step.

Finally, as we've suggested, the rising rates of ADHD also strongly suggest that we review and reconfigure an educational system that increasingly has tied children's success at school to performance on high-stakes standardized tests. This prevalent pressure to constantly rate and track and measure our children is part of a bigger trend toward more competitive, hurried, and unsatisfying lives. It hits home with particular poignancy when you think back to the fact that four in 10 high school seniors at several affluent California schools have taken prescription stimulants as study aids, even as hospital admissions from adverse effects of the medications continue to rise.

Children with and without ADHD deserve better schools, teachers, and educational policies, to accommodate individual learning styles and replace our current narrow focus on results from standardized tests with more humane and innovative strategies to encourage their talents and eagerness to learn. We're all for high academic standards, including the Common Core, but high-test-scores-or-bust policies contribute to unintended bad outcomes, such as fast-rising ADHD diagnoses among the nation's poorest children.

The good news here is that accommodations designed for kids who are restless and easily bored usually end up bringing out the best in their classmates as well. Such changes might include less rote homework, more positive reinforcement, more physical activity built into the day, and more out-of-the-chair activities, such as teamwork on projects. Note that we're not advocating for a permissive set of open classrooms. Children with ADHD, and most children in general, do best when warmth, understanding, and encouragement are matched by high expectations and structure.

What Would Some Sensible, Evidence-Based Policies Look Like to Prevent Overdiagnosis and Underdiagnosis and Most Effectively Cope with ADHD?

The evidence clearly supports the fact that many American children today are being wrongly diagnosed with and/or over-medicated for ADHD. One major study, published in the year 2000 in the *Journal of the American Academy of Child and Adolescent Psychiatry*, found that up to half of children receiving stimulant medications in a large sample from the Great Smoky Mountains region of the southeastern United States lacked a valid diagnosis of ADHD.

The trouble isn't in a lack of professional standards for assessments. Both the American Academy of Pediatrics and the American Academy of Child and Adolescent Psychiatry offer detailed guidelines for thorough evaluations. But most of the time, the guidelines are simply not followed. Instead, the all-too-common practice throughout the United States is a quick-and-dirty diagnosis in fewer than 15 minutes, which sadly results not only in grossly inflated diagnoses but also in many children who need treatment being missed.

The main problem is that the majority of psychologists who diagnose ADHD and of physicians who prescribe medication haven't been adequately trained, nor are they adequately reimbursed for careful monitoring. The incentives are mostly geared toward those short office visits and not for the thorough and multipart assessments that would draw in parents and teachers to offer perspectives on a child's performance outside of the doctor's office. All too often, incentives are also lacking for a doctor to keep track of how a child or adult is faring on a prescribed medication and whether side effects are discouraging its use. As for behavior therapy, which should be a key part of treatment for children, incentives are nearly nil, given that few insurance companies reimburse for it and insufficient numbers of professionals are trained in it.

Beyond the problem of bad diagnoses is that of poorly conceived policies that have encouraged many people without a genuine disorder to seek a diagnosis to qualify for accommodations in school or for national tests. Colleges and testing firms need to set more rigorous standards about who can qualify for special privileges. One interesting solution is to allow accommodations for anyone requesting them—but then officially indicate that their test scores have been obtained with accommodations. At least in this scenario, there would be not be the current "run" on accommodations that never get noted in test-score reports.

As a model for future standards of diagnosis, we are impressed by the Kaiser Permanente health maintenance organization's ADHD Best Practices Committee, for the HMO's Northern California region. For the past two decades, leading physicians and psychologists in that group have established and followed their own high-quality set of rules for evidence-based evaluations and treatments that take advantage of the special resources of the HMO, compared to private practitioners. For example, they recommend that pre-adolescent children be evaluated in a group with other kids, a much more natural environment than the usual setting of a clinician's office, surrounded by adults. The committee has also developed its own set of standardized forms for collecting information from teachers and parents. Best of all is that any child evaluated for ADHD is guaranteed to be seen not just by a psychologist or social worker or doctor limited to dispensing medication but also by a team that is qualified and trained to swiftly identify or rule out conditions that can mimic ADHD. Kaiser also offers parent coaching and behavior therapy as part of its plan, at least in some facilities.

Focusing On: The Future

The recent surge in ADHD diagnoses and treatment is quite likely to continue for at least several more years. The reasons are many, including recent loosening of diagnostic standards, continuing incentives including government financial aid and educational accommodations, the probable impacts of toxic pollution and teen pregnancies, and unrelenting global competitive pressures that are ramping up expectations in the classroom and on the job. Major pharmaceutical firms have also contributed to this trend, by funding ADHD research and aggressively advertising stimulant medications to not just mental health professionals but the general public. State and federal laws will continue to have strong (if mixed) effects. On the one hand, education policies tying performance on standardized tests to funding for schools, raising the pressure to identify and treat any laggards, have raised rates of ADHD diagnoses, particularly among children from families in poverty. But in recent years, state laws banning teachers from talking to parents about medication have slowed down the juggernaut, compared with what's happened in states without such laws. A question, however, is whether such laws exclude teachers from what could be valuable participation in the assessment process.

Growing awareness about female ADHD may contribute to the rising diagnoses in the near future, which could be beneficial for girls and women who historically have missed out on potentially valuable help. Yet overall, our modern epidemic of ADHD offers warning signs about harmful trends in our culture. One strong antidote could come from more and better training and adequate compensation of mental health professionals on the front lines. These practices, in turn, would help improve adherence to professional standards, focusing evidence-based treatment for people who genuinely need it while reducing the cursory diagnoses now fueling the ADHD epidemic.

RESOURCES

Recommended Books

Ashley, S. (2005). *The ADD and ADHD Answer Book: Professional Answers to 275 of the Top Questions Parents Ask*. Naperville, IL: Sourcebooks.

Barkley, R. A. (2000). *Taking Charge of ADHD: The Complete, Authoritative Guide for Parents*. New York, NY: Guilford Press.

Barkley, R. A. (2012). *Executive Functions: What They Are, How They Work, and Why They Evolved*. New York, NY: Guilford Press.

Barkley, R. A. (2013). *Defiant Children: A Clinician's Manual for Assessment and Parent Training*. New York, NY: Guilford Press.

Barkley, R. A. (Ed.). (2015). *Attention Deficit Hyperactivity Disorder: A Handbook for Diagnosis and Treatment* (4th ed.). New York, NY: Guilford Press.

Beauchaine, T. P., & Hinshaw, S. P. (2013). *Child and Adolescent Psychopathology* (2nd ed.). Hoboken, NJ: Wiley.

Beauchaine, T. P., & Hinshaw, S. P. (Eds.). (2015). *Oxford Handbook of Externalizing Spectrum Disorders*. New York, NY: Oxford University Press.

Brown, T. E. (2013). *A New Understanding of ADHD in Children and Adults: Executive Function Deficits*. New York, NY: Routledge.

Brown, T. E. (2014). *Smart but Stuck: Emotions in Teens and Adults with ADHD*. San Francisco, CA: Jossey-Bass/Wiley.

Denevi, T. (2014). *Hyper: A Personal History of ADHD*. New York, NY: Simon & Schuster.

Ellison, K. (2010). *Buzz: A Year of Paying Attention*. New York, NY: Hyperion Voice.

Greene, R. (2005). *The Explosive Child: Understanding and Helping Easily Frustrated, "Chronically Inflexible" Children*. New York, NY: Harper Paperbacks.

Hallowell, E., & Jensen, P. S. (2010). *Superparenting for ADD: An Innovative Approach to Raising Your Distracted Child*. New York, NY: Ballantine.

Hallowell, E., & Ratey, J. (2011). *Driven to Distraction: Recognizing and Coping with Attention Deficit Disorder* (Rev. ed.). New York, NY: Anchor.

Harris, J. R. (1998). *The Nurture Assumption: Why Children Turn Out the Way They Do*. New York, NY: The Free Press.

Hinshaw, S. P. (2007). *The Mark of Shame: Stigma of Mental illness and an Agenda for Change*. New York, NY: Oxford University Press.

Hinshaw, S. P. (2009). *The Triple Bind: Saving Our Teenage Girls From Today's Pressures*. New York, NY: Ballantine.

Hinshaw, S. P., & Scheffler, R. M. (2014). *The ADHD Explosion: Myths, Medication, Money, and Today's Push for Performance*. New York, NY: Oxford University Press.

Mate, G. (1999). *Scattered: How Attention Deficit Disorder Originates and What You Can Do About It*. New York, NY: Penguin.

Mischel, W. (2014). *The Marshmallow Test: Mastering Self-Control*. New York, NY: Little, Brown.

Monastra, V. J. (2005). *Parenting Children With ADHD: 10 Lessons That Medicine Cannot Teach*. Washington, DC: American Psychological Association.

Nadeau, K. G., Littman, E. B., & Quinn, P. O. (2015). *Understanding Girls With ADHD* (2nd ed). Washington, DC: Advantage Books.

Neven, R. S., Anderson, V., & Godber, T. (2002). *Rethinking ADHD: Integrated Approaches to Helping Children at Home and School*. Crows Nest, Australia: Allen & Unwin.

Newmark, S. D. (2010). *ADHD Without Drugs: A Guide to the Natural Care of Children With ADHD*. Tucson, AZ: Nurtured Heart.

Nigg, J. T. (2006). *What Causes ADHD: Understanding What Goes Wrong and Why*. New York, NY: Guilford Press.

Pera, G. (2008). *Is It You, Me, or Adult A.D.D.? Stopping the Roller Coaster When Someone You Love Has Attention Deficit Disorder*. San Francisco, CA: 101 Alarm Press.

Pfiffner, L. J. (2011). *All About ADHD: The Complete Practical Guide for Classroom Teachers* (2nd ed.). New York, NY: Scholastic Professional Books.

Power, T. J., Karustis, J. L., & Habboushe, D. F. (2001). *Homework Success for Children With ADHD: A Family-School Intervention Program.* New York, NY: Guilford Press.

Quinn, P. (2011). *100 Questions and Answers About Attention Deficit Hyperactivity (ADHD) in Women and Girls.* Sudbury, MA: Quinn & Bartlett.

Ratey, J. J., with Hagerman, E. (2008). *Spark: The Revolutionary New Science of Exercise and the Brain.* New York, NY: Little, Brown.

Rose, L. T., with Ellison, K. (2013). *Square Peg: My Story and What It Means for Raising Innovators, Visionaries, and Out-of-the-Box Thinkers.* New York, NY: Hyperion.

Safren, S. A., Sprich, S., Perlman, C. A., & Otto, M. W. (2005). *Mastering Your Adult ADHD: A Cognitive-Behavioral Treatment Program.* New York, NY: Oxford University Press.

Solanto, M. V. (2011). *Cognitive-Behavioral Therapy for Adult ADHD: Targeting Executive Dysfunction.* New York, NY: Guilford Press.

Sparrow, E. P., & Erhardt, D. (2014). *Essentials of ADHD Assessment for Children and Adolescents.* Hoboken, NJ: Wiley.

Taylor, B. E. S. (2007) *ADHD and Me: What I Learned From Lighting Fires at the Dinner Table.* Oakland, CA: New Harbinger.

Taylor, J. F. (2006). *The Survival Guide for Kids With ADD or ADHD.* Minneapolis, MN: Free Spirit.

Tuckman, A. (2009). *More Attention, Less Deficit: Success Strategies for Adults With ADHD.* Plantation, FL: Specialty Press.

Wilens, T. E. (2008). *Straight Talk About Psychiatric Medications for Kids* (3rd ed.). New York, NY: Guilford Press.

Wright, S. D. (2014). *ADHD Coaching Matters: The Definitive Guide.* College Station, TX: ACO Books.

Journals That Feature Primary Research Articles About ADHD

ADHD Attention-Deficit and Hyperactivity Disorders
JAMA Psychiatry
Journal of Abnormal Child Psychology
Journal of Attention Disorders
Journal of Child Psychology and Psychiatry
Journal of Clinical Child and Adolescent Psychology
Journal of Consulting and Clinical Psychology
Journal of the American Academy of Child and Adolescent Psychiatry

Internet Resources

Centers for Disease Control: http://www.cdc.gov/ncbddd/adhd/

National Institute of Mental Health: http://www.nimh.nih.gov/
health/publications/attention-deficit-hyperactivity-disorder/
index.shtml

Children and Adults with Attention-Deficit/Hyperactivity Disorder
(CHADD), offering news about the advocacy group and articles of
interest: https://www.google.com/webhp?sourceid=chrome-
instant&ion=1&espv=2&ie=UTF-8#q=chadd

ADDitude Magazine online (CHADD's national magazine): http://
www.additudemag.com/index.html/

National Resource Center on ADHD (a project of CHADD): http://
www.help4adhd.org/

ADHD Coaches Organization: http://www.adhdcoaches.org/

American Academy of Child and Adolescent Psychiatry Provider
Finder: http://www.aacap.org/AACAP/Families_and_Youth/
Resources/CAP_Finder.aspx

INDEX

Abikoff, Howard, 128–129
Abuse, 56–57, 70
Academic pressure. *See* Performance pressure
Academics, effects of ADHD on, 66–67, 69
Accidents, 70–71, 83
Accountability, 168–170
Acupuncture, 157
ADD. *See* Attention deficit disorder
Adderall, 96, 114, 168
Additives, 135–136
ADHD Best Practices Committee, 174–175
ADHD Coaches Organization, 157
The ADHD Explosion (Hinshaw and Scheffler), 86
ADHD industrial complex. *See* Industrial complex
ADHD Without Drugs (Newmark), 140
Adolescents, 69–71, 107–108
Adoptive parents, 36
Adults. *See also* Age
  continuing growth in rate of diagnosis and, 163
diagnosis and, 43
symptoms and presentation in, 71–72
taking medicines, 95–96
Advertising, 18, 166–167
Affection, parental, 34
Affordable Care Act, 165
African Americans, 84
AFTA. *See* Saudi ADHD Society
Age, xvii. *See also* Adolescents; Adults; Children
Age of Enlightenment, 20
Air pollution, 172
Alcohol abuse, 60, 70
Alcohol exposure, 28
All About ADHD (Pfiffner), 127
Allergies, 58
Alzheimer's disease, 152
Ambiguity, xvi
Amen, Daniel, 151–152
American Academy of Child and Adolescent Psychiatry, 53–54, 173
American Academy of Pediatrics, 53–54, 136, 164, 173
American Occupational Therapy Association, 160
American Psychiatric Association, 106, 138

American Society of Health-
System Pharmacists, 112
Amphetamines, 96, 97, 99
Ancestry, 25–27
Antidepressants, 96
Anxiety disorders, 54–56, 59
APD. *See* Auditory processing
disorder
Appetite, 102
Arithmetic pill, 97
Armodafinil, 96
Artificial colors, 136
Aspirin, 139
Assessment. *See* Diagnosis
Atomoxetine, 101, 103
Attachment patterns, 33–34
Attention, ADHD as deficit
of, 8–10
Attention deficit disorder
(ADD), 11–12
Auditory processing disorder
(APD), 55–56
Authoritarian parenting, 34–35
Authoritative parenting,
34, 123
Autism, 10–11, 19–20, 27, 80

Balance boards, 150
Barkley, Russell, 9, 122
Behavioral impulsivity, 80
Behavior modification, 120–121
Behavior therapy
benefits of, 109
cognitive-behavior therapy, 109,
129–130
direct contingency
management, 120–121
effectiveness of, 100
lack of incentives for, 174
with medications, 130–131
for organization, 128–129
overview of, 119–120, 131–132
parent-training programs,
121–125

social skills groups, 127–128
use at school, 125–129
Benzedrine, 97
Bertin, Mark, 159
Biofeedback, 140–143, 155–156,
160–161
Biofeedback Certification
International Alliance, 161
Biology, context and, xxii
Bipolar disorder, 55
Birthweight, 27, 29, 86, 164–165
Bishop, Dorothy, 150–151
Bisphenol A, 28–29
Blood pressure medications,
101–102
Blue light, 41
Bradley, Charles, 97
Brain injuries, 58
Brains
exercise and, 134
gender and, 79
medications and, 98–99
medications and development
of, 103–104
overview of in people with
ADHD, 30–32
Brain scans, diagnostic, 151–152
Brain waves, 49. *See also*
Neurofeedback
Brazil, 117
Breggin, Peter, 105–106
Brown, Thomas E., 98
Bulimia, 70
Bupropion, 96
Burning, 83
Bush, George W., 18

Caffeine, 100
"Call of Duty," 40
Calvinism, 105
CAM. *See* Complementary and
alternative medicine
Campbell, Susan, 35
Car accidents, 70–71, 83

Cardiac issues, 102
Carrey, Jim, 170
Cartoons, 39–40
Carville, James, 170
Catapres, 101–102
Causes of ADHD
    within brains, 30–32
    environmental, 27–28
    inherited, 25–27
    overview of, 41–42
    parents and, 33–37
    schools, academic pressures
        and, 37–38
    video games, social media, and
        other screen entertainment
        as, 38–41
CBT. See Cognitive-behavior
    therapy
CD. See Conduct disorder
Center for the Difficult Child, 145
Central auditory processing
    disorder, 55–56
Cerebellum, 150
CHADD. See Children and
    Adults with Attention Deficit
    Disorder
Checklists, 46
Chelation, 157
Chemical exposure, 28, 172
Child abuse, 56–57
Children, 65–69, 164
Children and Adults with
    Attention Deficit Disorder
    (CHADD), 17, 105, 106, 166
China, 90, 116
Church of Scientology, 105–106
Cigarettes, 28, 60, 70
Citizens Commission on Human
    Rights, 105–106
Cliques, 67
Clonidine, 101–102, 103
Coaching, 156–157
Coffee, 100
Cogmed, 155

Cognitive-behavior therapy
    (CBT), 109, 129–130
Cognitive enhancement, 113–114
Cognitive impulsivity, 80
Colorado State Board of
    Education, 169
Combined presentation, 5
Common Core, 173
Comorbid conditions, 58–61,
    170, xxii
Complementary and alternative
    medicine (CAM), 157–158
Computer training programs,
    154–156
Concerta, 96, 116. See also
    Methylphenidate
Conduct disorder (CD), 59, 80
Conflicts, 10
Conflicts of interest, 51
Consequences of ADHD,
    12, 81–83
Consequential accountability, 87–
    88
Consumers, strategies for, 149,
    159–161
Context, 75–76, xxii
Control, ADHD as lack of, 8–10
Controversy
    attraction of, 49
    Diagnostic and Statistical Manual
        and, 51
    overview of, xix–xx, xv–xvi
    Ritalin Wars, 104–106
Cortex development, 31–32
Costs of untreated ADHD, xviii
Crichton, Alexander, 20–21
Cultural implications of current
    diagnosis rates, 171–173
Cutting, 83

Daily report cards (DRC),
    125–126, 147
Darwin, Charles, 73
Daytrana, 168

DDAT. *See* Dyslexia dyspraxia attention treatment
Definition of ADHD, 3–4
Delayed gratification, 8–10
Demand shock, 165–166
Dementia, 152
Dependency, 112–113
Depression, 55, 70
Desperate Housewives, 115
Developmental-behavioral pediatricians, 43
Developmental histories, 47
Deviancy training, 127
Dexedrine, 96, 100
Dextroamphetamine, 100
DHA. *See* Docosahexaenoic acid
Diagnosis
  co-existing conditions and, 58–61
  continuing growth in rate of, 163–166
  differential, 54–58
  differing rates among states, 86–88
  of inattentive form of ADHD, 61–62
  increasing rates of, 16–20, 85–86, xv
  lack of objective assessment for, 49–50
  neuropsychological testing for, 52–53
  obtaining best possible, 62–63
  persons qualified to perform, 44–45
  prevalence vs., 15–16
  process for, 45–49
  professional guidelines for, 53–54
  racial and economic groups and, 84–86
  reasons for evaluation and, 43–44
  statistics on, xv

varying rates in nations outside of U.S., 88–89
Diagnostic and Statistical Manual (DSM)
  continuing growth in rate of diagnosis and, 164
  diagnosis and, 45–46, 48
  name in, 12
  overview of, 50–52
  symptoms listed in, 5–6
Diagnostic brain scans, 151–152
Diet, 135–137
Differential diagnosis, 54–58
Direct contingency management, 120–121
Direct-to-consumer (DTC) ads, 167
Disorganization, as symptom, 4–5
Docosahexaenoic acid (DHA), 139
Doctors. *See* Pediatricians; Psychiatrists; Psychologists
Dolphins, swimming with, 157
Dopamine
  brain function and, 30–31
  fatty acids and, 138
  heritability and, 26
  medications and, 98, 107
  receptors, 31
Dore, Wynford, 150
Dore Program, 150–151
Douglas, Virginia, 11–12
DRC. *See* Daily report cards
DRD_{4-7} allele, 26, 35, 73–74
Driving, 70–71, 83
Drug abuse, 60, 70, 113–115
Drugs. *See* Medications; Supplements
DSM. *See* Diagnostic and Statistical Manual
DTC ads. *See* Direct-to-consumer (DTC) ads
Dynevor Limited, 151
Dyslexia, 55–56

Dyslexia dyspraxia attention
treatment (DDAT), 150–151

Eating disorders, 70
Economics, 84–86, 89–90, xviii
Education, 23, 85. *See also* Schools
Education for All Handicapped
Children Act, 85
EEG. *See* Electroencephalograms
EEG feedback. *See* Neurofeedback
Eicosapentaenoic acid (EPA), 139
Einstein, Albert, 74–75
Electroencephalograms (EEG), 49.
See also Neurofeedback
Elimination diet, 136
Ellison, Katherine, xxi
Encephalitis, 22–23
Endocrine disruptors, 29
Endorphins, 134
Environment, impacts of,
27–28, 33–41
EPA. *See* Eicosapentaenoic acid
Essential fatty acids, 138
Eugeroics, 96
Eustulic, 101–102
Executive functions, problems
with, 6–7
Exercise, 133–134
Externalizing behavioral
problems, 80
Eyberg, Sheila, 123

Facebook, 166, 167–168
Family conflict, 68–69
Family-focused therapy,
treatments and, 143–145
Farah, Martha, 152
Fatty acids, 137–138
Feingold, Benjamin, 135
Feingold diet, 135–136
Females. *See* Gender
Fernandez, Melanie A., 123
Ferritin, 140
Fetal alcohol effects, 28

"Fidgety Phil" description, 22
Fish, 138
Fish oil capsules, 139
504 Plans, 146
fMRI. *See* Functional magnetic
resonance imaging
Focalin, 96
Food and Drug Administration,
167, 168
Friendships, 68
Frontal lobe, 31, 101
Functional magnetic resonance
imaging (fMRI), 32

Gender
adolescence and, 70
diagnosis and, 19
need for greater understanding
of ADHD in girls and
women and, 170–171
rates and, 79–80
stigma and, xvi
symptoms and presentation
and, 80–81
trauma and, 56
video games and, 40
Gene-environment
interaction, 27, 29
Gene expression, 27, 35
Generalized anxiety disorder, 54
Genes, 26, 27, 73–74. *See also*
Inherited causes of ADHD
Gift theory, 73–75
Gingko biloba, 139
Ginseng, 139
Glasser, Howard, 145
Goodman-Beatty, Michelle, 168
Graduated licensing system,
70–71, 83
"Grand Theft Auto," 40, 49
Gratification, delayed, 8–10
Greece, ancient, 20
Guanfacine, 101–102, 103
Guendelman, Maya, 56

Habit-forming medications, 112–113
Hallowell, Edward, 34, 75, 122
Harris, Judith Rich, 33
Head Start programs, 145
Healthgrades, 63
Health-impaired conditions, 85
Heart rate, 102
Heavy metal exposure, 28
Heritability, 25–27
Hilton, Paris, 170
Hinshaw, Stephen, 34, 83, 86, xxi
History of ADHD, 20–24
HKD. *See* Hyperkinetic disorder
Hoffman, Heinrich, 22
Huffman, Felicity, 115
Hunter-gatherers, 73
Hyperactive/impulsive presentation, 5
Hyperactivity, as symptom, 4–5
Hyperfocus, defined, 3
Hyperkinetic disorder (HKD), 51–52
Hyperkinetic impulse disorder, 23, 98
Hyperthyroidism, 57
Hyperverbal behavior, 171
Hypothyroidism, 57

ICD. *See International Classification of Diseases*
IDEA. *See* Individuals with Disabilities Education Act
identified Patient (IP), 143
Imaging studies, 32, 151–152
Impulsivity, 4–5, 7, 80. *See also* Self-control
Inattention, as symptom, 4–5
Inattentive presentation, 5, 61–62, 82
Incentives, 174
India, 89–90

Individuals with Disabilities Education Act (IDEA), 17, 85, 146–147
Industrial complex (ADHD), 137–140
being a smart consumer and, 159–161
coaching, 156–157
computer training programs, 154–156
marijuana and, 153–154
mindfulness practices and, 158–159
occupational therapists and, 159
overview of, 149, 161, xix–xx
schemes to avoid, 150–152
usefulness of, 157
Inherited causes of ADHD, 25–27
Insecure attachment, 33–34
Insomnia, 57
Insurance, 165
Intelligence quotient (IQ) tests, 53
Internalizing behavioral problems, 80, 83
International Classification of Diseases (ICD), 51–52, 88
International Dyslexia Association, 150
International Society for Neurofeedback and Research, 156
Intuniv, 101–102
IP. *See* Identified Patients
IQ tests, 53
Iron, 140
Israel, 90

James, William, 21
Janssen Pharmaceuticals, Inc., 116
Jensen, Peter, 122
JetBlue, 74

Kaiser Permanente health maintenance organization, 174–175
Karolinska Institute, 155
Kinko's, 74
Klingberg, Torkel, 155

Latinos Americans, 84, 86
Lead exposure, 28, 29
Learned helplessness, 69
Learning and processing disorders, 55–56, 59
Learning Curve, 155
Life coaching, 156–157
Light, sleep patterns and, 41
Limbic ADHD, 152
Lobbyists, 17

Magnesium, 140
Magnetic resonance imaging, functional, 32
Males. See Gender
Manic-depressive illness, 55
Marijuana, 153–154
Marshmallow test, 8
Massage, 157
Math disorder, 55–56
Matthews, Sheila, 169
MBD. See Minimal brain dysfunction
McNeil Pediatrics, 167
Meany, Michael, 34
Medicaid, 17, 85, 87
Medical marijuana, 153–154
MediCann, 153–154
Medications. See also Pharmaceutical companies; Stimulants; Supplements
    abuse of in people without disorder, 113–116
    advertising and, 18
    with behavior therapy, 130–131
    brain development and, 103–104

dependency and abuse risks and, 112–113
duration of benefits of, 106–107
earliest, 16–17
economics and, 89–90
function of, 98–101
funding for, 85
gender and, 82
history of use of, 97–98
improving chances of effectiveness of, 110–111
monitoring treatment with, 108–110
most common in use, 96–97
non-stimulant, 101–102
number of people taking, 95–96
in other countries, 116–117
overview of, 117–118
pediatricians and, 43
reasons teens stop taking, 107–108
side effects of, 99, 102–103
statistics on, xvi–xvii
substance abuse risk and, 111–112
Meditation, 158–159
Memory, 6, 101, 155
Mentors, 144–145
Mercury exposure, 29, 138
Metadate, 96
Methylphenidate, 16–17, 96, 98, 99. See also Ritalin
Military service, 75
Mindfulness meditation, 158–159
Mindfulness Research Center, 158
Minerals, 140
Minimal brain dysfunction (MBD), 23, 97–98
Mischel, Walter, 8
Modafinil, 96–97, 103
Mood disorders, 55, 59
Motivation, deficit of, 9
Mozart, Wolfgang Amadeus, 74–75

MTA. *See* Multimodal Treatment
   Study of Children
   with ADHD
Multimodal Treatment Study of
   Children with ADHD (MTA),
   99–100, 130–131
Music classes, 157

N-acetyl cysteine (NAC), 139–140
Nagging, 36
Name of ADHD, 11–12
Narcolepsy, 57
National Institute of Mental
   Health (NIMH), 142
National Survey of Children's
   Health, 18, 79
Naturalistic research, 112
Natural selection, 73
Neeleman, David, 74, 170
Neurofeedback, 140–143, 155–156,
   160–161
Neurons, 30, 98–99
Neuroprotective effects, 104
Neuropsychological testing, 52–53
Neurotransmitters, 26, 30, 98,
   99, 138
Newmark, Sanford, 140
Nicotine exposure, 28
NIMH. *See* National Institute of
   Mental Health
No Child Left Behind Law,
   18, 87–88
Norepinephrine (noradrenaline),
   30, 98, 101
Novartis, 106
Novelty seeking, 73
The Nurture Assumption
   (Harris), 33
Nurtured Heart Approach, 145
Nutrition, 135–137
Nuvigil, 96

Obama, Barack, 88
Obesity, 134

Obsessive-compulsive disorder
   (OCD), 54
Occupational therapists, 159
ODD. *See* Oppositional defiant
   disorder
Off-label prescriptions, 96–97
Omega-3 fatty acids, 137–138
Onset, age of, 3, 16
Oppositional defiant disorder
   (ODD), 59, 80
Orfalea, Paul, 74
Organizational skills, 10, 128–129
Organophosphate exposure, 28
Orphanages, 33–34
Outdoor play, 133–134
Overdiagnosis
   causes of, 15, 19, 47, 166–167
   cultural implications of,
      171–173
   overview of, xix
Owens, Dee, 113–114
Oz, Dr., 139

Parent-child interaction therapy
   (PCIT), 123–125
Parent management, 121–125
Parents, 33–37, 68–69, 121–125
Parent-training programs,
   121–125
Parkinson's disease, 30
Pathology, 51
PCIT. *See* Parent-child interaction
   therapy
Pediatricians, 43, 53–54
Performance pressure
   as cause for increase in
      diagnosis rate, 163, xvii–
      xviii, xxi
   causes of ADHD and, 37–38
   in China and India, 89–90, 116
   stimulant use in people
      without ADHD and, 113–115
Permissive parenting, 34
Pfiffner, Linda, 127

Pharmaceutical companies, 51, 166–168
Pharmaceutical treatments. *See* Medications
Phelps, Michael, 74, 170
Phobias, 54
Phthalates, 28–29
"A Picture is Worth a Thousand Dollars" (Farah), 152
Plastics, 28–29
"Play Attention" systems, 155–156
Pneumoencephalograms, 97
Policies, 18, 86–88, 168–170, 173–175
Positive illusory bias, 73
Posner, Michael, 34–35
Postencephalitic behavior disorder, 23
Post-traumatic stress disorder (PTSD), 54
Poverty, 84–86
Pregnancy, medications and, 103
Premature birth, 27, 29
Preschoolers, 164
Presentations of ADHD, 5. *See also* Symptoms and presentation
Preservatives, 135–136
Pressure. *See* Performance pressure
Prevalence. *See also* Diagnosis
  autism and, 19–20
  historical, 20–24
  increasing rates of, 16–20, 85–86, xv
  overview of, 15–16
Provigil, 96
Psychiatrists, 43–44
Psychologists, 43–44, 174
Psychopharmacologic Calvinism, 105
Psychosis, 153
Psychotherapy. *See* Behavior therapy

PTSD. *See* Post-traumatic stress disorder

Quinnell, Scott, 151

Race, diagnosis and, 84–86
Race to the Top, 88
Rappaport, Judith, 100
RateMDs.com, 63
Ratey, John, 134
Ratey, Nancy, 156–157
Rehabilitation Act of 1973, 146
Report cards, daily, 125–126, 147
Resilience, 76
Resting state brain activity, 32
Results of ADHD. *See* Consequences of ADHD
Reuptake, 99
Ring of Fire ADHD, 152
Risk factors. *See* Causes of ADHD
Risk-taking, 26, 35
Ritalin, 96, 98, 104–106, 116, 169. *See also* Methylphenidate
Ritalin Wars, 104–106

Saudi ADHD Society (AFTA), 116
Saudi Arabia, 116
Scans, 151–152
Scheffler, Richard, 86, xxi
Schemes. *See* Industrial complex
Schizophrenia, 153
School funding policies, 18, 86–88
Schools. *See also* Education; Performance pressure
  academic support from, 145–147
  behavior therapy at, 125–129
  causes of ADHD and, 37–38
  diagnosis and, 46–47
  need for changes in, 172
  policies and pressures of, xxiii
  reasons for increased symptoms at, 48–49
Scientology, 105–106

Scripts, 129
SCT. *See* Sluggish cognitive tempo
Section 504 policies, 146
Seizure disorders, 58
Selective attention, 8
Selective norepinephrine
    reuptake inhibitors
    (SNRI), 101
Self-control, ADHD as lack
    of, 8–10
Self-destructive behavior, 83
Self-employment, 75
Self-esteem, 72–73
"The Selling of Attention Deficit
    Disorder," 167
Sensory integration issues,
    159, 160
Sensory processing disorder, 60–61
Serotonin, 138
Sexual activity, 70
Sexually transmitted diseases, 70
Shaw, Philip, 31
Shire, 168
Single-photon emission
    computerized tomography
    (SPECT) scans, 151–152
Skepticism. *See* Controversy
Skin conditions, 97
Sleep apnea, 57
Sleep disorders, 41, 57, 102
Sleepy-minded, 26, 100
Sluggish cognitive tempo
    (SCT), 62
SmartBrain Technologies, 155
Smart pills, 113–116
Smith, Matthew, 169
Smoking, 28, 60, 70
SNRI. *See* Selective
    norepinephrine reuptake
    inhibitors
Social life, consequences of
    ADHD to, 67–68
Social media, 38–41
Social skills groups, 127–128

Socioeconomic status, 84–86
Sodium benzoate, 136
*Spark: The Revolutionary New
    Science of Exercise and the
    Brain* (Ratey), 134
Spectrum disorder, ADHD
    as, 3–4
SPECT scans, 151–152
SpongeBob SquarePants, 39
SSI. *See* Supplemental
    Security Income
Standardized testing, 86–87, 172
State policies, 18, 86–88, 168–170
States, differing diagnosis rates
    among, 86–88
Sterman, M. Barry, 142
Stevens-Johnson syndrome, 97
Stigma, 15, 84–85, xvi
Still, George, 21–22
Stimulants. *See also* Medications
    abuse of, 113–115
    anxiety disorders and, 55
    function of, 98–101
    most common in use, 96–97
    number of people taking, 95
    reason for success as
        treatment, 26
St. Johns wort, 157
Strattera, 101
Subsistence nations, 89
Substance abuse, 58, 59–60,
    111–112, 168
Sugar, 137
Suicide, 83
Super-parenting, 34
Superparenting for ADD
    (Hallowell and Jensen), 122
Supplemental Security Income
    (SSI), 17, 85
Supplements, 137–140, 157
Surveys, 18–19
Sustained attention, 8
Symptoms and presentation
    adolescence and, 69–71

adulthood and, 71–72
  best context and, 75–76
  in earliest years of life, 65–66
  gender and, 80–81
  grade school and, 66–69
  overview of, 4–7, 77–78
  positive aspects of, 73–74
  resilience and, 77
  self-esteem and, 72–73
  typical characteristics of
    children vs., 10–11
Synapses, 30, 98–99

Talking Back to Ritalin (Breggin),
  105–106
Talk therapy, 130
Tannock, Rosemary, 49
Teenagers. *See* Adolescents
Teicher, Martin, 50
Television, 38–41
Tenex, 101–102
Testing. *See* Diagnosis
Thyroid imbalances, 57
Time management skills, 10
Tolchinsky, Anatol, 40
Tolerance, 109
Tourette syndrome, 59
Transporters, 99
Trauma, 56
Treatments. *See also* Behavior
  therapy; Family therapy;
  Industrial complex;
  Medications; Supplements
  best forms of, 130–131
  computer training programs,
    154–156
  diet and, 135–137
  exercise, 133–134
  family-focused, 143–145
  neurofeedback, 140–143

  overview of, 148
Tyrosine, 139

Under-arousal, 26, 100
Underdiagnosis
  gender and, 3, 79, 81–83, xvi
  prevalence and, 15
  stigma and, xix
Understanding Girls with AD/HD
  (Nadeau et al), 83
Unique Logic and
  Technology, 155
United Kingdom Food Standards
  Agency, 136
Unproven treatments. *See*
  Industrial complex
Untreated ADHD, costs of, xviii

Victorian Age, 21
Video games, 38–41
Vigilance-promoting drugs, 96
Violent media, 40–41
Vitamins, 140
Vive program, 144–145
Volkow, Nora, 9, 31
Vyvanse, 96, 168

Water pollution, 172
Wellbutrin, 96
Willpower, ADHD as lack of, 8–10
Women. *See* Gender
Work, reasons for increased
  symptoms at, 48–49
Working memory, 6, 101, 155

Yelp, 63

Zinc, 140
"Zombie" misconception,
  100–101, 105–106